The Scope of Political Theology

The Scope of
Political Theology

Edited by Alistair Kee

SCM PRESS LTD

Petro Keeling
amico carissimo
qui rerum spiritualium
ut ita dicam tot pocula
mecum compotor exhausit

No attempt has been made to make the extracts
in this book typographically consistent. In all cases,
the spelling and punctuation etc. of the original
publisher have been used.

334 01463 8

First published 1978
by SCM Press Ltd, 58 Bloomsbury Street London WC1

Filmset by Richard Clay Ltd
and printed in Great Britain by Fletcher & Son Ltd, Norwich

Contents

Preface

When, some years ago, I first began to teach a course in political theology, I discovered that there was no convenient collection of texts and no introduction to the movement itself. From this need emerged *A Reader in Political Theology*, first published by SCM Press in 1974 and recently revised. That book traced a linear development in political theology from 1966 to 1974. I was also aware of a broad spectrum of examples of political theology in different parts of the world. This present collection attempts to reflect the breadth, or scope, of political theology today.

The structure of the book facilitates its use by those who wish to become acquainted with particular types. However, the structure might also be misleading. For example, I do not wish to suggest that Asian theologians can only be considered in a special chapter devoted to the theology of that continent. For this reason I have included a piece by Balasuriya in the chapter on spirituality and a contribution by Koyama on mission. Bonino and Miranda might have contributed to 'Politicized Theology' and Fierro might have been included in the first chapter. One feature of the present collection, however, fails to underline these interconnections. The women theologians appear only in the chapter on 'Feminist Perspectives'. No doubt I shall be taken to task for this, with the usual accusations. The alternative would have been worse, namely, to include women in other chapters simply to show that they write as well as men. I looked carefully in the hope of finding a suitable contribution from a feminist theologian for the first chapter. And for a piece by Rosemary Ruether, who has included ecology among the many subjects she has written about. But in the end I had to trust my judgment and risk the criticism.

John Robinson once told me there were two things he would never do. The first I do not now recall (!) but the second was to edit a book. A wise decision. The finished work looks very professional, thanks to the tireless work of Margaret Lydamore. But on the cutting-room floor lie several million words which could not be used, silent but awesome witness to what Freud called 'the omnipotence of thought' in Christianity.

ALISTAIR KEE

Torr na Faire
March 1978

1 · Political Theology

It has been said that you can recognize a metaphysical question because it induces a certain vertigo. Perhaps the phrase 'political theology' has the same effect. Politics we know about, and religion: indeed it is apparently a basic civil right not only to hold opinions on all matters concerning politics and religion, but to express them with confidence and at length. But the phrase indicates some strange alchemy by which oil and water have been mixed. It is after all a common view – shared by people with nothing else in common – that we must not mix religion and politics. The two sides are agreed on this much.

There is first of all the claim that we must keep politics out of religion. That seems obvious enough, until we reflect that throughout the entire history of Europe, politics and religion have been constantly and inextricably bound together. On closer inspection the call to keep politics out of religion is an innovation. On closer inspection still, it appears to be inconsistent, for it transpires that normally it is only *some* forms of politics that are to be excluded.

Historically the politics of the right have been conservative, preserving the existing order and defending it against its enemies. The political right has not needed an explicit theory to justify its position. That obligation has always been for those of the left, those who advocate change. For most of its history, the Christian church has been associated with the political right. With exceptions, the general Constantinian position has been that the church assumes responsibility for preserving not only order but the existing basis of order.

Nor was this position adopted after great debate and heartsearching. It was a position adopted quite unconsciously and until recently it has been almost unchallenged. The integration of conservative political theory and religion seems perfectly 'natural'. As part of the political right, no justification has been offered: the obligation lies with those who propose to alter the historical arrangement. Those who claim that politics must be kept out of religion would therefore be more consistent if they acknowledged that religion has traditionally been under the influence of conservative political thinking.

To exemplify this relationship, we take the unlikely case of F. D. Maurice. He is often called 'the father of Christian socialism', a title so inappropriate as to be almost ironic. His position is summed up by Torben Christensen. 'He wished to say that monarchs mirrored and were witness to the divine kingship of Christ. The significance of aristocracy was that it displayed the humanity of the spirit as the ruling part in man over his animal grovelling nature. As this humanity was the gift of Christ, aristocracy thus bore witness to His divine humanity which was characterised by His self-sacrifice for his poorer brethren. Monarchy and aristocracy thus belonged to the Divine Order. To abolish them and introduce Democracy, which Maurice always understood as the government of self-will, was consequently tantamount to denying God and His constituted universe and robbing men of the witness of the unchangeable laws in God's dealing with mankind' (*Origin and History of Christian Socialism 1848–54*, Universitetsforlaget, Aarhus 1962).

The point is not that Maurice provided a theological justification for the *status quo* and opposition to Chartism but rather that he claimed his theology was based on the revealed truth of the Bible and Christian tradition. Those who advocate the separation of politics from religion would do well to reflect on how conservative political assumptions have already infiltrated theology.

But secondly, on the other side of the coin, are those who claim that we must keep religion out of politics. There is no lack of examples in history of the blatant intervention of religion – or religious leaders – into politics. At the beginning of the fourteenth century, the Pope appeared as one monarch in Europe among many. True, his armies were not so strong as some but he had a terrifying weapon. He could use religious sanctions to achieve political ends. 'In Innocent III the papacy reached the summit of its worldly power' (W. Walker, *A History of the Christian Church*, Scribners, NY 1959). An example from nearer our own time comes from Cuba at the time of the Castro revolution. Leslie Dewart asks: 'How did the Cuban Church come to so conceive itself and its relations to the secular world that the question whether the revolution was or was not communist became the only matter worth judging?' (*Christianity and Revolution: The Lesson of Cuba*, Herder

& Herder, NY 1963). Here the Catholic hierarchy simply aligned themselves in the Cold War with the West. No religious criteria were applied.

Keep religion out of politics: religious leaders must not act in purely political ways under the cloak of religion. But to be consistent there is another and perhaps more important sense in which this phrase might be used. For convenience it might be called 'political messianism'. Not the intervention of religion into politics so much as the appropriation by politics of religious attitudes and claims. This of course was precisely the issue which faced the early church in the imperial cult, *Caesar Kyrios*. The effect was to bind men to Caesar – body and soul. In this sense, keeping religion out of politics means setting limits to the demands of the state. An example of this deliberate blurring of the lines between religion and politics is found in a statement by Goebbels in 1936 after a broadcast by Hitler. 'When the Führer addressed his last appeal to the people, it was as if a profound agitation went through the whole nation; one felt that Germany was transformed into a single House of God, in which its intercessor stood before the throne of the Almighty to bear witness ... It seemed to us that this cry to heaven of a people for freedom and peace could not die away unheard. That was religion in its profoundest and most mystical sense. A nation then acknowledged God through its spokesman, and laid its destiny and its life with full confidence in his hand' ('Memorandum submitted to Chancellor Hitler' by the leaders of the German Evangelical Church, in A. C. Cochrane, *The Church's Confession under Hitler*, Westminster Press, Philadelphia 1962). In the modern world there are still examples of the blatant intervention of religion into politics, but the far greater danger is posed by political messianism.

The separation of politics and religion is a common enough cry but as we have seen it is remarkably inconsistent in application. Those who would keep politics out of religion adopt this position only to protect the existing alliance of politics and religion. Those who urge religion to stay out of politics may well do so to clear the ground for their own messianic pretentions. Neither side wishes separation, merely advantage. In this sense those who advocate political theology are at least more consistent. Political theology does not arise from opportunism or the attempt to win a strategic advantage, but from a particular understanding of the way we can be true to the fundamental character of Christian faith, not least the biblical faith.

The meaning of the phrase 'political theology' is not self-evident. It can be used by left or right. The Russian anarchist, Michael Bakunin, could use it a century ago, while fifty years ago, as used by Carl Schmid, it served a more conservative movement. But the contemporary meaning is not governed by such precedents. It stems from the work of J. B. Metz. The meaning of the phrase should be allowed to emerge from the perspectives and concerns of the kind of writings exemplified in this collection.

Johannes B. Metz · *The Privatization of Religion*

Johannes B. Metz, *Theology of the World*, Herder & Herder, NY 1969, pp.107–15. First published in *Theology of Renewal*, Proceedings of the Congress on the Theology of Renewal, ed. L. K. Shook. Used by permission of the Pontifical Institute of Mediaeval Studies, Toronto, and the author.

I understand political theology, first of all, to be a critical correction of present-day theology inasmuch as this theology shows an extreme privatizing tendency (a tendency, that is, to center upon the private person rather than 'public,' 'political' society). At the same time, I understand this political theology to be a positive attempt to formulate the eschatological message under the conditions of our present society.

1. Let me first explain the function of political theology as a *critical corrective* of modern theology. I shall begin with a few *historical reflections*.

The unity and coordination of religion and society, of religious and societal existence, in former times acknowledged as an unquestionable reality, shattered as early as the beginning of the Enlightenment in France. This was the first time that the Christian religion appeared to be a particular phenomenon within a pluralistic milieu. Thus its absolute claim to universality seemed to be historically conditioned. This problematic situation is also the immediate foundation of the critique developed by the Enlightenment and, later, by Marxism. From the beginning this critique took on the shape in which it still appears today. It approaches religion as an ideology, seeking to unmask it as a function, as the ideological superstructure of definite societal usages and power structures. The religious subject is being denounced as a false consciousness, that is, it is viewed as an element of society which has not yet become aware of itself. If a theology seeks to meet such a critique, it must uncover the socio-political implications of its ideas and notions. Now – and here I am conscious of daring simplification – classic metaphysical theology failed to discharge its responsibilities in this quarrel. The reason is that its notions and categories were all founded upon the supposition that there is no problem between religion and society, between faith and societal practice. As long as this supposition was true, it was indeed possible for a purely metaphysical interpretation of religion to be societally relevant, such as was the case, for instance, in the Middle Ages with its great theologians. However, when this unity was broken, this metaphysical theology got itself into a radical crisis as the theoretical attorney in the pending case between the Christian message of salvation and sociopolitical reality.

The prevailing theology of recent years, a theology of transcendental, existential personalist orientation, is well aware of the problematic situation created by the Enlightenment. We might even say that, in a certain sense, it originated as a reaction against this situation. Still this reaction was not direct and sustained: the societal dimension of the Christian message was not given its proper importance but, implicitly or explicitly, treated as a secondary matter. In short, the message was 'privatized' and the practice of faith reduced to the timeless decision of the person. This theology sought to solve its problem, a problem born of the Enlightenment, by eliminating it. It did not pass through the Enlightenment, but jumped over it and thought thus to be done with it. The religious consciousness formed by this theology attributes but a shadowy existence to the sociopolitical reality. The categories most prominent in this theology are the categories of the intimate, the private, the apolitical sphere. It is true that these theologians strongly emphasize charity and all that belongs to the field of interpersonal relations; yet, from the beginning, and as though there were no questions, they regard charity only as a private virtue with no political relevance; it is a virtue of the I-Thou relation, extending to the field of interpersonal encounter, or at best to charity on the scale of the neighbourhood. The category of encounter is predominant; the proper religious way of speaking is the interpersonal address; the dimension of proper religious experience is the apex of free subjectivity, of the individual or the indisposable, the silent center of the I-Thou relation. It seems clear then that the forms of transcendental existential and personalist theology, currently predominant, have one thing in common: a trend towards the private.

I should like to cast further light on this tendency which I have called a privatizing tendency. Let us look at the results of modern *Formgeschichte* and the way they are interpreted by modern theology. It is well known that the Gospels' intention is not to present a biography of Jesus in the current sense of the word; their account of Jesus does not belong to the genus of private biography, but to the genus of public proclamation – of kerygma – which is the form in which the Christian message of salvation couches its assertions. The exegetical studies in so-called *Formgeschichte* have shown that the Gospels are a multi-layered text in which the message is proclaimed in the aforesaid way. Now it seems to me that it was, in a certain sense, a fateful event when the discoveries and conclusions of *Formgeschichte* were at once interpreted in the categories of theological existentialism and personalism. This meant that the understanding of the kerygma was immediately limited to the intimate sphere of the person; briefly, it was privatized. Its word was taken merely as a word addressed to the person, as God's personal self-communication, not as a promise given to men, to society. The hermeneutics of the existential interpretation of the New Testament proceeds within the closed circuit of the I-Thou relation. Hence the necessity to deprivatize critically the understanding of the datum of our theology. *The deprivatizing of theology is the primary critical task of political theology.*

This deprivatizing, it seems to me, is in a way as important as the program of demythologizing. At least it should have a place with a legitimate demythologizing. Otherwise there is a danger of relating God and salvation to the existential problem of the person, of reducing them to the scale of the person, and so of downgrading the eschatological kerygma to a symbolic paraphrase of the metaphysical questionableness of man and his personal private decisions.

No doubt there is an emphasis on the individual in the message of the New Testament. We might even say that it is the gist of this message – especially in its Pauline expression – to place the individual before God. When we insist on deprivatizing, we do not in the least object to this orientation. On the contrary, for it is our contention that theology, precisely because of its privatizing tendency, is apt to miss the individual in his real existence. Today this existence is to a very great extent entangled in societal vicissitudes; so any existential and personal theology that does not understand existence as a political problem in the widest sense of the word, must inevitably restrict its considerations to an abstraction.

A further danger of such a theology is that, failing to exercise its critical and controlling function, it delivers faith up to modern ideologies in the area of societal and political theory. Finally, an ecclesiastical religion, formed in the light of such a privatizing theology, will tend more and more to be a 'rule without ruling power, a decision without deciding power. It will be a rule for those who are willing to accept it, so long as no one gives it a knock; it will not be a rule inasmuch as no other impulse will proceed from it but the impulse to self-reproduction (A. Gehlen).

2. With this, the *positive task* of political theology comes to light. It is, to determine anew the relation between religion and society, between Church and societal 'publicness,' between eschatological faith and societal life; and, it should be added, 'determine' is not used here in a 'pre-critical' sense – that is, with the intention of *a priori* identifying these two realities – but 'post-critically' in the sense of a *'second reflection.'* Theology, insofar as it is political theology, is obliged to establish this 'second degree reflection,' when it comes to formulate the eschatological message under the conditions of the present situation of society. Hence let me briefly describe the characteristics both of this situation, that is, how it should be understood, and of the biblical message, which is the determining factor of this theological political reflection.

(a) I shall explain the situation from which today's theological reflection takes its *starting point,* by referring to a problem raised by the Enlightenment and which, at least since Marx, has become unavoidable. This problem may, in an abbreviated formula, be presented thus: according to Kant, a man is enlightened only when he has the freedom to make public use of his reason in all affairs. Hence the realization of this enlightenment is never a merely theoretical problem, but essentially a political one, a problem of societal conduct. In other words, it is linked with such socio-political suppositions as render enlightenment possible. Only he is enlightened who, *at the same time*, fights to realize those socio-political presuppositions that offer the possibility of publicly using reason. When, therefore, reason aims at political freedom and, consequently, theoretical transcendental reason appears within practical reason, rather than the reverse, a deprivatization of reason is absolutely necessary. Every 'pure' theory, whether it be stressed or even over-stressed, is nothing but a relapse into a pre-critical consciousness. For it is clear that the subject's critical claims cannot be sustained as 'mere' theory. A new relation between theory and practice, between knowledge and morality, between reflection and revolution, will have to be worked out, and it will have to determine theological thought, if theological thought is not to be left at a pre-critical stage. Henceforth, practical and, in the widest sense of the word, political reason must take part in all critical reflections in theology. More and more, practical political reason will be the center of the classical discussion of the relation between *fides* and *ratio*, and the problem of the responsibility of faith will find the key to its solution, again, in practical public reason. Properly speaking, the so-called fundamental hermeneutic problem of theology is not the problem of how systematic theology stands in relation to historical theology, how dogma stands in relation to history, but what is the relation between theory and practice, between understanding the faith and social practice. If the task of political reflection in theology, as emerging from the present situation, is to be characterized summarily, it might best be done in the way we have just indicated. This also shows that our intention is not, once again, to mix faith and 'politics' in a reactionary manner. Rather, it is to actualize the critical potential of faith in regard to society.

(*b*) *Biblical tradition*, in its turn, obliges us to undertake this 'second reflection' on the relation between eschatological faith and societal action. Why? Because salvation, the object of the Christian faith in hope, is not private salvation. Its proclamation forced Jesus into a moral conflict with the public powers of his time. His cross is not found in the intimacy of the individual, personal heart, nor in the sanctuary of a purely religious devotion. It is erected beyond these protected and separated precincts, 'outside,' as the theology of the Epistle to the Hebrews tells us. The curtain of the temple is torn forever. The scandal and the promise of this salvation are public matters. This 'publicness' cannot be retracted nor dissolved, nor can it be attenuated. It is a recognizable fact attending the message of salvation as it moves through history. In the service of this message, Christian religion has been charged with a public responsibility to criticize and to liberate. 'All the authors of the New Testament' – I am quoting the well-known biblical scholar, H. Schlier – 'are convinced that Christ is not a private person and the Church is not a private association. They tell us of Christ's and his witnesses' encounter with the political world and its authorities. None of them has given more fundamental importance to this aspect of the history of Jesus than the apostle John. To him it is a lawsuit, which the world, represented by the Jews, brings against Jesus and his witnesses. This suit was brought to its public judicial conclusion before Pontius Pilate, the representative of the Roman Empire and the holder of the political power.' Provided it is not read with the eyes of Bultmann, John's account of the passion is organized around this scene. The scene before Pilate is heavy with symbolism.

Political theology seeks to make contemporary theologians aware that a trial is pending between the eschatological message of Jesus and the socio-political reality. It insists on the permanent relation to the world inherent in the salvation merited by Jesus, a relation not to be understood in a natural-cosmological but in a socio-political sense; that is, as a critical, liberating force in regard to the social world and its historical process.

It is impossible to privatize the eschatological promises of biblical tradition: liberty, peace, justice, reconciliation. Again and again they force us to assume our responsibilities towards society. No doubt, these promises cannot simply be identified with any condition of society, however we may determine and describe it from our point of view. The history of Christianity has had enough experience of such direct identification and direct 'politifications' of the Christian promises. In such cases, however, the 'eschatological proviso,' which makes every historically real status of society appear to be provisional, was being abandoned. Note that I say 'provisional,' not 'arbitrary.' This eschatological proviso does not mean that the present condition of society is not valid. It *is* valid, but in the 'eschatological meanwhile.' It does not bring about a negative but a critical attitude to the societal present. Its promises are not an empty horizon of religious expectations; neither are they only a regulative idea. They are, rather, a critical liberating imperative for our present times. These promises stimulate and appeal to us to make them a reality in the present historical condition and, in this way, to verify them – for we must 'veri-fy' them. The New Testament community knew at once that it was called to live out the coming promise under the conditions of what was their 'now,' and so to overcome the world. Living in accord with the promise of peace and justice implies an ever-renewed, ever-changing work in the 'now' of our historical existence. This brings us, forces us, to an ever-renewed, critical liberating position in face of the extant conditions of the society in which we live. Jesus' parables – to mention another biblical detail in this context – are parables of the kingdom of God, but, *at the same time*, they instruct us in a renewed critical relationship to our world. *Every eschatological theology, therefore, must become a political theology, that is, a (socio-)critical theology.*

Jürgen Moltmann · *Political Theology of the Cross*

Jürgen Moltmann, *The Crucified God*, Harper & Row, NY, and SCM Press 1974, pp. 136–37, 143–45, 317–18, 328–29

The theological conflict between Jesus and the contemporary understanding of the law can explain his rejection as a 'blasphemer', and in some circumstances his condemnation by the Sanhedrin, if such a trial is historical, but does not explain his execution by crucifixion. Jesus did not undergo the punishment for blasphemy, which in Israel at his time, as can be seen from the death of Stephen, was always that of stoning. Jesus was crucified by the Roman occupying power.

According to Roman law, crucifixion was a punishment for escaped slaves, as we know from the revolt of Spartacus and the crucifixion of more than 7,000 slaves on the *Via Appia*. It was also a punishment for rebels against the *Imperium Romanum*, as is shown by the many crucified resistance fighters after the revolts in Israel had been crushed. Crucifixion was a punishment for crimes against the state, and not part of general criminal jurisdiction. To this extent, one can say that crucifixion at that time was a political punishment for rebellion against the social and political order of the *Imperium Romanum*.

The spread of the *Imperium Romanum* was associated with the idea of the *Pax Romana*, and the *Pax Romana* in its turn was associated, in spite of all the religious tolerance which we know the Romans to have exercised, with the compulsory recognition of the Roman emperor cult. The *Imperium Romanum* was a religious and political ordinance in the world of that time. In Israel the resultant setting up of Roman standards in the temple and the placing of the head of Caesar on the currency in circulation was consequently regarded by the 'zealots for the law' as a breach of the first commandment and therefore as an offence against religion which had to be resisted. It can be said, then, that Jesus was crucified by the Romans not merely for tactical and immediate political reasons of peace and good order in Jerusalem, but basically in the name of the state gods of Rome who assured the *Pax Romana*. In the societies of that time there was no politics without religion, any more than there was religion without politics. 'Jesus was condemned by Pilate as a political rebel, as a Zealot.' If we follow the historical conjectures of Oscar Cullmann, the

Roman cohorts whose duty was to protect the temple captured Jesus in Gethsemane. He was consequently from the first a prisoner of the Romans who, as the result of his appearances in Jerusalem, feared *stasis*, revolt. In this case, the hearing before the High Priest would rather have been a moral consultation which Pilate desired, in order to be certain that as a result of the execution of the supposed Zealot leader Jesus of Nazareth, the Jewish authorities and the Jewish people would not rise against him. The true trial, then, was a trial before Pilate, a political trial, made possible by the collusion of the Sanhedrin and Pilate. The inscription over the cross, the *titulus*, followed the practice of antiquity in naming the crime for which the punishment was given. It read: INRI – 'Jesus of Nazareth, King of the Jews'. As this *titulus* is recorded in the gospels, it can hardly be an invention of the Christian church, for it was too dangerous, and came into conflict with the terms which the Christian churches later sought with the *Imperium Romanum* in order to survive.

How can we explain the political fact that Jesus was crucified as a 'rebel' against the Roman Empire and as 'King of the Jews'? R. Bultmann states:

What is certain is merely that he was crucified by the Romans, and thus suffered the death of a political criminal. This death can scarcely be understood as an inherent and necessary consequence of his activity; rather it took place because his activity was misconstrued as a political activity. In that case it would have been – historically speaking – a meaningless fate.

But was he really no more than the victim of a misunderstanding and a meaningless fate? And if it was a misunderstanding, what brought it about? Was it merely a chance misunderstanding or an intrinsically necessary and inevitable misunderstanding? How otherwise could the Romans, afraid of revolt and anxious to maintain order, have understood Jesus? Is not their 'misunderstanding' on the same level as the 'misunderstanding' of him by the Pharisees? Did not even his own disciples 'misunderstand' him, as is shown by their flight from the cross? The simple distinction between religion and politics which Bultmann introduces when he speaks of his activity 'being misconstrued as a political activity' is nothing less than the projection back of the separation of religion and politics – religion is a private matter – from the bourgeois world of the nineteenth century, a separation which was sought only after a thousand years of conflicts between church and emperor, but has never yet been reached, even at the present day.

By regarding him as a Zealot rebel, Pilate certainly misunderstood Jesus, and because of his fear of a popular revolt was bound so to misunderstand him. But in the deeper sense of a challenge to the *Pax Romana* and its gods and laws, we can look back and realize that Pilate understood him aright. This is shown by the effect that the crucified man from Nazareth ultimately had upon the Roman Empire in the life of early Christianity. The worship of such a 'crucified God' contained a strictly political significance which cannot be sublimated into the religious sphere. The Christians' open rejection of emperor worship brought them martyrdom in a sense which was both religious and political. 'Since demons rule in the world, anyone who wishes to live there must show them veneration and submit to their ordinances. And therefore one must also submit to rulers, even if they demand that one takes an oath in their name. Through this belief Rome grew great, and it is not right to reject their gods and accept a god who is not even able to give his followers a patch of earth or a home, so that they have to slink about secretly in constant fear,' says Celsus. He accused the followers of the crucified Christ of rebellion (*stasis*). By their irreligiousness they were introducing revolt into the heavenly world amongst the gods and were therefore bringing revolt into the religious and political world on earth which corresponded to those gods. In an age in which politics and religion were one and, apart from domestic cults, could not be separated, it was scarcely possible for the activity of Jesus to be 'misconstrued as a political activity', as R. Bultmann supposes. The gospel of Jesus and his public behaviour were political in the extreme. He was bound to be understood as both religious and political, even if this did not mean that he himself was not understood as an object of faith. Consequently, he alienated both the anti-Roman Zealots and the anti-Jewish Romans. Both knew their business, the use of armed force as divine judgment, as was the custom in the world of that time. But Jesus interfered in this religious and political business to challenge and disrupt its rules, and 'had to be' removed.

Thus as a second theological dimension to the history of Jesus which led to his crucifixion as a 'rebel', we can definitely add the political dimension of the gospel of Jesus within a world in which religion and politics were inseparable.

If the one who was crucified in this way was raised up and

vindicated by God, as eschatological faith affirms, then this aspect too of the trial of Jesus must be recapitulated, and the faith which bears public testimony to it must draw upon the political dimension of his history. Christianity then poses the question, for resolution by open trial: Christ – or Caesar?

The theology of the cross is not 'pure theology' in a modern, non-political sense, or in the sense of private religion. Faith in the crucified Christ is in the political sense a public testimony to the freedom of Christ and the law of grace in the face of the political religions of nations, empires, races and classes. Between faith in Christ and the deified rulers of the world, the personal cults and the social and political fetishes of society, Jesus himself stands. The recollection of his crucifixion is something both dangerous and liberating.

In the Reformation, the theology of the cross was expounded as a criticism of the church; how can it now be realized as a criticism of society? If in the political trial of Jesus, the Caesar was the external reason for his end on the cross, how can the risen Christ become the internal reason for the end of Caesar?

If we attempt to draw the consequences of the theology of the cross for politics, the matter cannot be exhausted in general and abstract definitions of the relationship between church and state or dogmatic faith and political action. Concrete attention must be paid to religious problems of politics and to laws, compulsions and the vicious circles which for economic and social reasons constrict, oppress or make impossible the life of man and living humanity. The freedom of faith is lived out in political freedom. The freedom of faith therefore urges men on towards liberating actions, because it makes them painfully aware of suffering in situations of exploitation, oppression, alienation and captivity. The situation of the crucified God makes it clear that human situations where there is no freedom are vicious circles which must be broken through because they can be broken through in him. Those who take the way from freedom of faith to liberating action automatically find themselves co-operating with other freedom movements in God's history. Political hermeneutics calls especially for dialogue with socialist, humanistic and anti-racist movements. Political hermeneutics reflects the new situation of God in the inhuman situations of men, in order to break down the hierarchical relationships which deprive them of self-determination, and to help to develop their humanity. So there is need for critical solidarity with these movements; for

solidarity with them in the struggle against the forms of in-
humanity which threaten mankind; and for criticism and acceptance of criticism of the aims and methods of liberation. Political
hermeneutics of faith is not a reduction of the theology of the cross
to a political ideology, but an interpretation of it in political
discipleship. Political hermeneutics sets out to recognize the social
and economic influences on theological institutions and languages,
in order to bring their liberating content into the political dimension and to make them relevant towards really freeing men from
their misery in certain vicious circles. Political hermeneutics asks
not only what sense it makes to talk of God, but also what is
the function of such talk and what effect it has. Even here, none of
the so-called substance of faith is lost; rather, faith gains substance
in its political incarnations and overcomes its un-Christian abstraction, which keeps it far from the present situation of the crucified
God. Christian theology must be politically clear whether it is
disseminating faith or superstition.

If the Christ of God was executed in the name of the politico-
religious authorities of his time, then for the believer the higher
justification of these and similar authorities is removed. In that case
political rule can only be justified 'from below'. Wherever Christianity extends, the idea of the state changes. Political rule is no
longer accepted as God-given, but is understood as a task the
fulfilment of which must be constantly justified. The theory of the
state is no longer assertive thought, but justifying and critical
thought. The early church rejected the cult of the emperor and
replaced it with prayer for the emperor which represented a limita-
tion of his power. The Middle Ages and the Reformation relativized
political ordinances so that they became necessary ordinances in
the world, which served the well-being of people but not their
salvation. Puritanism abolished the feudal system and replaced it by
the covenant or the constitution of the free citizen. A critical political theology today must take this course of desacralization, relativi-
zation and democratization. If the churches become 'institutions for
the free criticism of society', they must necessarily overcome not
only private idolatry but also political idolatry, and extend human
freedom in the situation of the crucified God not only in the
overcoming of systems of psychological apathy, but also in the
overcoming of the mystique of political and religious systems of rule
which make men apathetic.

Christianity did not arise as a national or a class religion. As a dominant religion of rulers it must deny its origin in the crucified Christ and lose its identity. The crucified God is in fact a stateless and classless God. But that does not mean that he is an unpolitical God. He is the God of the poor, the oppressed and the humiliated. The rule of the Christ who was crucified for political reasons can only be extended through liberation from forms of rule which make men servile and apathetic and the political religions which give them stability. According to Paul, the perfection of his kingdom of freedom is to bring about the annihilation of all rule, authority and power, which are still unavoidable here, and at the same time to achieve the overcoming of equivalent apathy and alienation. Christians will seek to anticipate the future of Christ according to the measure of the possibilities available to them, by breaking down lordship and building up the political liveliness of each individual.

Alistair Kee · *Political Theology and Hermeneutics*

From an article in *Movement*, no. 29, SCM Publications, Dublin 1977.

In an age geared to selling the old product under a new name it might be thought that the phrase 'Political Theology' is simply new-improved high-speed theology's name for old fashioned 'Politics and Religion'. Indeed it would be comforting to think so. There is something puzzling and at the same time ominous about the phrase 'Political Theology'. It is not clear how we are to defuse it and render it harmless, smothered under the familiar clichés of politics and religion. We are much more at home with politics and religion. But the phrase 'Political Theology' suggests that while the familiar positions have been taken up in a continuing, if desultory, debate on politics and religion, somewhere or other the two spheres have been brought together in a new integration. Suddenly the protagonists in the old debate have found themselves upstaged and – what could not have been foreseen – now bound together in common opposition to the new threat. Like the Pharisees and the Herodians they must for the moment work together to dispose of this upstart before resuming their comfortable positions.

Political Theology has a negative as well as a positive function. It exposes false associations of religion and politics. It draws attention to political models and assumptions which have distorted the inter-

pretation of scripture and the development of Christian doctrine.
But it also goes on to indicate how a proper association of
politics and religion discloses directions for faith which are at once
hopeful and alarming. Three examples follow.

1. History as Revelation

The first example of the hermeneutical significance of political
theology concerns the historical nature of the biblical faith. To
anyone familiar with theology of the last 20 years the conjunction
of the words history/faith/revelation/bible must arouse an almost un-
controllable urge to rush for the door. A flood of books and
articles has reduced insight to cliché so that we can no more deny
the assertion than understand it. We are continually told that Christianity is a historical religion, that God has revealed himself in
history, yet the fact that we do not know what to make of this
is itself an example of the problem before us.

As Jeremiah had to break down before he could build, so
political theology has to make its own case by disposing of alternatives. Political theology maintains that God's revelation comes in
history. But does this distinguish it from any other type of theology?
It does if other types fail to take this statement seriously and find
a way of reducing its implications. The impression is often given that
God reveals himself and his purpose through the medium of history,
as if he could have chosen some other medium or, rejecting all
media, could have communicated it by theophany or verbal inspiration. It is in this sense that insight becomes a cliché and is
finally dissipated. We are not dealing with a timeless truth which is
posted to us, so to speak, through this particular slot in time. No,
here as elsewhere, the 'medium is the message'. The idea that there
is truth about life which can be discovered, abstracted from history
and presented in a timeless form is orthodox Idealism from Plato to
Hegel but it has nothing to do with Christian faith. As Assmann
says, *'Man's activity is de-politicized and de-historicized: it is no longer
an historical process.'* (*Practical Theology of Liberation*, Search Press
1975). Of crucial importance is Assmann's linking of the political
and the historical. Since in the Bible we are dealing with the
history of individuals, groups and nations the medium is not just
history in some neutral sense but politics. Politics is the locus of the
revelation and it is for this reason that insight has become cliché,
since theologians have in the main wished to 'purify' the truth
from this medium. But at the same time we must now recognize

that to try to de-politicize Christian faith is itself a political act of great importance.

There are various elements within Judaism which Christianity clearly does not fulfil, but if Christianity is seen in continuity with the faith of the Old Testament then it is in the prophetic/apocalyptic tradition. We shall come back to this point later but this tradition is characterized both by its concern for the political life of the people and also by its constant criticism of the order of the day. It is not difficult to see why theologians, who have been at the service of a Church which saw its duty to be the preservation of civil order, have therefore sought to de-historicize and de-politicize the faith. Nor is this to suggest any great conspiracy. For the most part these theologians belong (or come to belong) *'by kinship and sympathy to the bourgeois classes'* (W. Rauschenbush, *A Theology for the Social Gospel*, Abingdon Press, New York 1945) and pursue their work from that hermeneutical perspective. The prophetic tradition of the Old Testament would not allow religion to be divorced from politics, from the way people related to each other, from the ways in which nations dealt with each other. In the prophetic tradition we have a political theology, an integration of politics and religion which does not involve the overcoming of one side by the other. The prophet speaks without usurping the place of the king; he intervenes but without seeking to establish or strengthen his own personal position. There was of course in Judaism another tradition which sought to dehistoricize and depoliticize the religion of Israel, a tradition characterised by ritual and by law. Political theology therefore forces us to ask whether this movement within Christianity to dehistoricize and depoliticize it has not moved us away from the original prophetic/apocalyptic tradition towards the tradition of ritual and law. Where this movement is successful, whether in Christianity or Judaism, worship is evacuated of its political significance: it no longer dislocates men from their socio-political surroundings. The early church and the imperial rulers knew better than many modern scholars that worship can be an intensely political action. If not, then Rome would not have made such an issue of it. Sometimes new truth is old truth rediscovered at great cost. *'The time will shortly be upon us, if it is not already here, when the pursuit of contemplation becomes a strictly subversive activity'* (Daniel Berrigan, *America is Hard to Find*, SPCK 1973). Political theology therefore forces us to consider to what extent Christianity has been presented and understood from a hermeneutical standpoint quite foreign to it.

2. The Incarnation

In 1778 Lessing published a posthumous work by the late H.S. Reimarus, *Von dem Zwecke Jesu und seiner Jünger* and thereby set in motion what came to be called 'the quest of the historical Jesus'. In one sense it is a good example of a theological debate in its most 'pure' and a-political form, yet it is also an example of the hermeneutical question posed for us by political theology. There are different ways of stating the problem: we have two pictures (painted on glass) but do they correspond when one is set against the other? In what sense is the Christ of faith continuous with the historical Jesus? Not an unreasonable question surely and yet scholars have made heavy weather of the issue for 200 years. There seem to be three possibilities. The first is that the two pictures do indeed correspond. Yet throughout the Quest and latterly the New Quest there has been no agreement on how this is so. The second possibility is simply to deny the relevance of the problem, the approach in turn of Kierkegaard, Kähler, Barth and Bultmann. The danger is that if theologians disregard the question, others will draw their own conclusions from the failure. The third possibility is that implied by Reimarus himself, namely that there is no final correspondence between the two pictures. It is this possibility that political theology must analyse, a possibility which orthodox theologians cannot face, although they can provide no demonstration of correspondence.

How could the pictures diverge to such a degree? How could this carpenter be the architect of the world? How could the first born son of an obscure couple from Nazareth be the Second Person of the Trinity? How could this Jew, who believed David wrote the Psalms and Moses wrote the Pentateuch, be the inspiration of the Old Testament? How could his death, one of thousands ordered by a brutal but minor tyrant, have significance for Lao Tzu who died some 500 years before? Orthodoxy has claimed that no matter how, the two pictures are identical. Yet for 200 years scholars have been unable to make any advance on this dogmatic assertion. It may be that political theology has inadvertently hit on the solution. What if the original picture of Jesus has been de-historicized and de-politicized? This would mean that the Christ of faith would be related to the historical Jesus, but the two would not correspond. The 'transfiguration' is not simply one event in the gospel narratives, but rather the process by which the faith of the Church came to interpret and understand the significance of Jesus. The infancy narratives, the recognition at baptism, confession on the way to

Caesarea Philippi, entry into Jerusalem and post-resurrection commission: all of these elements indicate how faith transformed the
historical Jesus into the Lord of the church. It remains for political
theology to point out that in the same process of 'transfiguration'
there is also de-historicization and de-politicization. The interpretation of Jesus is written back into the accounts of his life and ministry
but unfortunately this interpretation is in a-historical and a-political
terms. Even in the synoptic gospels, from beginning to end Jesus is
no longer the Master whom the disciples followed and never
understood, but a supernatural figure, both Christ and Son of Man.
The revelation is therefore from a supernatural source and is finally
the revelation of the significance of his death.

But in this we see the repetition of what has already been
said in more general terms about the failure of theologians to take
seriously the historical element in the biblical faith. Just as we said
at that time the medium is the message, that history cannot be
boiled away to distil some timeless truth, so now we must say that
if there is revelation in Jesus then his life is the medium and also
the message. How could it ever be to our advantage to be increasingly removed from the incarnation of God's grace and truth?
But this is precisely what happens when Jesus is set aside in favour
of an a-historical confession of faith in him.

The other side of this particular coin is that once the historical
Jesus is de-historicized then we are free to say whatever seems
appropriate to us about the exalted Christ. That is, the historical
Jesus no longer acts as a criterion of the truth. The historical Jesus
says that no rich man shall enter the Kingdom, but apparently the
Christ of faith imposes no such distasteful restriction. The historical
Jesus does not protect himself, but the Christ of faith is involved
in every crusade whether against Moors or Communists. Small
wonder the two pictures fail to coincide. With the historical Jesus
out of the way theologians have been able to call upon Christ the
Warrior (thought by some to be the Prince of Peace) as an ally in
the theology of domination.

There is an ironic twist to this story in recent years. Christians
who have been involved in liberation movements – and many more
who have never been involved in anything at all – have sought to
legitimize their cause by that modernizing assertion, 'If Jesus were
alive today he would be a revolutionary', or 'Jesus was a revolutionary in his own time'. Now of course it may be that Jesus was a
Zealot supporter or even the leader of his own revolutionary
movement. We shall never know, because the Jesus of the gospels

has been de-politicized. As Moltmann says, *'The ministry of Jesus could have been non-political only if it had been concerned with ineffective inner dispositions.'* (*The Crucified God*, SCM Press 1974). But of course the dehistoricized faith is concerned only with such narrowly 'religious' matters. The depoliticized Jesus, who is said to fulfill the most politicized religious tradition in the history of the world, has apparently little or nothing to say on the great issues of the day which would have been taken up and transformed by any of the Classical Prophets. By an extraordinary tour de force the gospel writers maintain that there was no political significance whatsoever in the circumstances surrounding the arrest, trial(s), torture, condemnation and public execution of Jesus. Revolutionaries look in vain for incidents or words from the gospels to lend direct support to their cause. The theologians of the religious establishment are more fortunate: if the depoliticized Jesus does not speak against them, then he must be for them.

The hermeneutical implications of all this are very important but behind the whole issue lies something even more fundamental. In all this there is implied a certain doctrine of God. Political theology raises the question whether the doctrine of God has ever been christianized.

3. The Incarnate God

It was Bonhoeffer who first called for a fundamental re-examination of the doctrine of God in modern theology. While in the 1960s many philosophers and theologians asked about the viability of the doctrine of God it was Bonhoeffer 30 years ago who asked rather about the appropriateness of the doctrine. Of all the doctrines of Christianity we may say that this is the one which has proved most resistant to christianization. It has been formed from many different sources but we may doubt if it is fundamentally and coherently Christian.

There are still elements of the primitive Hebrew God under contract to do battle with the gods of other nations, alongside more sophisticated Babylonian conceptions of the God who created the universe. There is the unpredictable God of wrath who strikes down innocent followers, who condemned Paul and terrorized Luther. Yet there is also the God, more like an oriental mother than a father, who cares for his people in their troubles. There is the God who is so jealous of his righteousness that he will have nothing to do with sinners and there is the God who sends his only Son to die for them. There is the God who can shout like a drunk man or burst into peals of laughter but there is the God who is changeless and unmoved by the things of this veil of tears. All of these elements and many more are found in what is loosely called the Christian doctrine of God. They presumably bear witness to the varied experiences of the devout throughout the ages, but since they are not all mutually compatible we must ask what is the criterion by which this grab-bag of divine attributes can be sifted and be made to yield a specifically Christian picture of God. With this we return to our last section: the criterion must be Jesus, the historical Jesus in whose life, ministry and death certain things come to light. And certainly Jesus must provide a negative criterion for a Christian doctrine of God: nothing can be Christian which is incompatible with what comes to expression in him.

When Christians focus attention on the historical events surrounding the life of Jesus of Nazareth they can begin from one of two different directions. Either the God who is already known is seen to act in these events, or these events reveal God in a qualitatively new way. Traditionally the emphasis has been on the former. The God already known (and therefore by definition pre-Christian) acts in these events. How he acts is determined by what was already known of him. The events themselves have not been allowed to cause any fundamental change in the understanding of God. But if this is so then, ironically, the Jewish God of history has been dehistoricized, that is, he is no longer being revealed by historical events. Hence the difficulty of Christian theologians in discovering anything in the teaching of Jesus which distinguishes him from contemporary Jewish thinkers. The revelation in this view is not taking place in the life of Jesus at all (history is no longer the medium) but in the death and resurrection. But to speak in this way is to place the revelation beyond history into a metaphysical (in the pejorative sense) dimension which tells us nothing at all about our socio-political lives. How could it be otherwise: if the Christ of faith is already dehistoricized and depoliticized inevitably the God who was in Christ is dehistoricized and depoliticized. Theology is then free to continue to make statements about God that are not compatible with the historical Jesus. For example, given that God cannot simply forgive sinners, the revelation is that Christ died for the sins of the world. But it is precisely this 'given' which is incompatible with the life and teaching of Jesus. He justifies his own association with sinners and his own offer of forgiveness simply by claiming that God acts in his way. But if this is so, then what is revealed in Jesus must be something rather different – and more profound. *'Can one still understand the crucified Christ on the presupposition of a concept of God imported "from elsewhere"? On the contrary, must one not understand this "God the Father of Jesus Christ" completely in the light of what happened on the cross?'* (J. Moltmann, *The Crucified God*).

Political theology therefore calls us to look for the revelation in history – actually in history – and not in some metaphysical sphere beyond it. It calls us to pay attention to what is brought to light without rushing too quickly to see what light is thrown on old problems which perhaps are false problems in the first place. Political theology therefore offers a new hermeneutical standpoint from which to understand both the life of Jesus and his death.

According to the traditional doctrine of God, Christ for a time 'emptied himself, taking the form of a slave'. But because of his obedience God has exalted him, which we take to mean that Christ has been restored to glory again. This means that the pre-Christian understanding of God is maintained throughout, indeed it is confirmed because the implication is that God is certainly not revealed in Jesus. The implication is that God could not be revealed in Jesus because Jesus lacks the glory of God. Such a view could only be maintained if the revelation were considered to be in the efficacy of the death of Christ. But if we are serious about God revealed in history, if we are serious about God in Christ, about incarnation, then we must say that God is revealed in weakness, in defeat, disgrace and scorn. *'God is not greater than he is in this humiliation. God is not more glorious than he is in this self-surrender. God is not more powerful than he is in this helplessness. God is not more divine than he is in this humanity.'* (Moltmann, op. cit.)

Now here is something new, that no contemporary Jew would ever have dared to say. And here is something of the most astounding political significance, that the new life and power that God promises is not given to the wise and powerful who control the world and manipulate it to their own ends. Nor is it given to their house-prophets who assure them that religion has nothing to do with politics. From this new hermeneutical standpoint it is alarming to see how undeclared or unconscious political attitudes have been at work in Biblical exegesis, the formation of dogma and social ethics.

2 · Politicized Theology

During the Highland Clearances, the vacuuming of the Scottish glens to make ready for the sheep which were to be more profitable to the clan chiefs than the poor kinsmen ever could be, a minister of the Kirk would sometimes accompany those who served the eviction notices. At the sight of the cloth the miserable families were more likely to go quietly into exile. The church has always been ready to help the poor. In 1977 the South African Army College in Voortrekkerhoogte received its first ever group of young clergymen reporting for National Service. They are no longer exempt from compulsory military service. The church has always been loyal to the state, with spiritual encouragement and the Nine Commandments. The theology of the church has also been at the service of the state and the ruling class.

By 'politicized theology', a rather brutal use of English, I wish to refer to theology which itself has undergone a certain traumatic transformation. The starting point is that type of theology which is commonly encountered, whether in university faculties or in seminaries throughout the world. It purports to be politically neutral, concerned with other matters. But it is precisely this theology which legitimates the present order of things and distracts the attention of students from other elements both in the Bible and in the tradition. A few examples, did I hear? Amos taught not justice-then-cult, but justice-instead-of-cult. For effect, it is claimed. The author of the Epistle to the Hebrews taught the end of sacrifice. Chalices are continually raised. Jesus was not stoned as a prophet but executed as a messiah. A plot: a mistake. Münzer is of greater interest to Marxists than Christians. And well rid of him. The Son of Man had no bed for the night, but Keble is more influential than Ludlow.

The first step is the realization that theology is anything but neutral. It is very selective, preferring historical research to contemporary issues, individual piety to social problems. Many of those who take this step leave the church: if they are clergy then they take up secular jobs. It is not easy to see how theology can be radically altered.

The second step occurs when the theologian himself becomes more politically or socially radical. He can now clearly see that theology has been used by conservative forces and he speaks out against them. But it is his new political consciousness that enables him to speak. His theology is unchanged. This was the position in Europe a decade ago during a brief outburst of political radicalism within the church. Apart from emotive claims that Jesus was a revolutionary the theology of the politically conscious was still largely unchanged. On a larger scale this is the position throughout Latin America. There is no lack of theologians who can match words, and sometimes deeds, with their Marxist partners, but whose theology is strangely unexamined. It is very often inherited pietism or unreconstructed dogma learnt in the seminary. The fact that the Marxist analysis is pronounced by a priest does not make it theology.

A third stage, which really does not mark progress, is to blame those who taught this theology in the first place. 'Don't forgive them, Lord, for they *do* know what they are doing.' But in fact the teachers of theology may still be quite oblivious to the influences upon them in their understanding of the subject. However, if a young theologian complains bitterly enough he may be invited to teach a course on 'Church and Society', a Friday afternoon option offered in the summer term. In recent years there has been a good deal of criticism of European theology from Latin American writers. Naturally they have been invited on lecture tours in the United States and Europe. The most sensitive of their former teachers would like to know just where Europe went wrong. It may seem rather juvenile to them to be told that precisely because they are European they would not understand.

Although this third stage is understandable it does not develop the second stage very far. A fourth stage attempts to change the content of theology but the theology of liberation has been rather disappointing on its theological side. Exodus is an ever popular starting point. For those who manage to progress into the New Testament the Magnificat and the Beatitudes are suggestive. But somehow it is all *ad hominem*, an attempt to state what is widely talked about, in terms which will enlist the sympathy of Christians who might be frightened off if they heard it in its original Marxist form. The promised 'liberation of theology' just does not arise from this procedure. It takes two forms. The first is a sifting through the Bible to see how the Bible actually said two thousand years ago what the political radicals are now saying. If there was such a metaphor I should say this activity is locking the stable door after someone else has both captured the horse and bolted the door. It is unlikely that this approach will do justice to the Bible: it will certainly not fool the comrades. The other procedure is to choose another series of biblical passages to criticize church structures. This may initiate a brief but lively debate within the church, or precipitate disciplinary action. In neither case does this Oedipal attack change anything. 'Father Gonzales is revolutionary, you know.' (Thinks: 'Do not call any man on earth "father" ... The greatest among you must be your servant.')

Both in Europe and Latin America we are entering a fifth stage. The intransigence of traditional theology and the minimal success in reforming it suggests that the problem must be traced back to an ontological level. The suspicion dawns that up till now the radical theologian, for all his intemperate rejection of the old ways, must at some fundamental level be in full agreement with the traditional approach. If Assmann represents the second stage, Bonino the third and Segundo the fourth, then Dussel is moving out towards the fifth. I do not agree with his analysis, but then that has not been the criterion for making the selections for this book. He identifies the problem as an ontological one, but reverts to the third stage by typifying the problematic approach as European. There is some evidence of a new approach in Germany, Holland and of course Spain: Europe cannot be regarded as uniformly reactionary. Nor can Latin American theology be held up at this moment in time as the breakthrough for which we had hoped.

As we have noted, the second stage is characterized by a combination of political radicalism and religious conservatism, described by Fierro as 'leftist orthodoxy'. Even the Marxist-Christian Dialogue and subsequent ongoing contact between Marxists and Christians (or those who claimed to be both) has not led to a radical transformation of theology. If there is to be a further development then theology must incorporate the social consciousness provided by a Marxist perspective. This does not mean becoming Marxist: to the contrary Marxism will be seen for what it is, yet another reductionist cul de sac. Ironically the social consciousness brought about by Marx makes it necessary to reject the ideology which has been constructed upon it and which is not the only option open. 'Political theology is the specific and proper form of theology in an epoch dominated by Marx', as Fierro claims. It could be argued that Marx is closer to the Judaeo-Christian tradition than was Aristotle. But in any case Marx is no more accepted here uncritically than was Aristotle by Thomas.

The effect of all this is that theology must be done not simply in the context of a call for revolution, a call which is quite meaningless in Europe and North America, but rather in awareness of the present level of development of our culture. We can hardly proceed with a sophisticated awareness of the nature of this culture at a political level and a pre-critical pietistic awareness at the religious level. Two main concerns of theology since the 1950s have been secular theology and political theology. We now see the beginnings of their convergence. Secular theology took seriously the need for radical changes in theology but was politically naive about the culture in which theology is now done. Political theology has far too long been radical about the culture without taking seriously the problems raised, rightly, by the culture for traditional theology. The urgency of this new theology concerns not only Europe. As Fierro notes, the more successful the political revolution in Latin America, the sooner will appear a culture in which traditional pietism and orthodoxy will be eccentric.

Juan Luis Segundo · *The Ideological Infiltration of Dogma*

Juan Luis Segundo, *The Liberation of Theology*, Orbis Books, Maryknoll and Gill & Macmillan 1977, pp.40–44

We must not underestimate Christian common sense as it has been applied to certain ambiguous things in the Church – to the *sacraments*, for example. It is quite obvious to most people that Masses, baptisms, and weddings – in short, the basic parish activities – consume most of the time, money, energy, and personnel of the Catholic Church. Now in the last chapter we came to see that a liberative theology must of necessity be an historical theology grounded on the questions that well up from the present. It cannot simply drag out metaphysical or universal questions that have been handed down from generation to generation by long tradition. Thus simple logic tells us that only a Christian community that is keenly sensitive to history can provide the basis for such a liberative theology. Attention to the signs of the time is the theological criterion which sets off a theology of liberation from a conservative, academic theology.

But the fact is that the concept of 'sacrament' which filters through the concrete praxis of the Church is the image (or better, the idol) of an *ahistorical* sacred efficacy. Everyone is perfectly aware that in most ordinary cases Sunday Mass is the only bond relating the average Christian to God. This Mass is characterized by unvarying liturgical elements, pre-established readings, an unchanging Eucharistic service, and the eternal return of the same feasts on the yearly liturgical calendar. In short, it constitutes the polar opposite of a religion based on historical sensitivity. Except in minor details, the Sunday Mass remains the same before and after a general disaster, an international crisis, and a thoroughgoing revolution.

What does that mean? To the majority of Christians it undoubtedly means that God is more interested in nontemporal things than in solutions for the historical problems that are cropping up. And it is too much to ask the average Christian, who is subjected to such strong theoretical and practical pressure, to detach his scale of values from what seems to be the religious realm *par excellence* in order to associate it with another type of activity in the name of Christianity itself.

This situation is heightened by the desperate pleas of the Church for unity – for *sacramental* unity of course. However, the average Christian is well aware that the people gathered to receive a given sacrament share nothing with each other except their need to receive it. Wherein lies the decisive importance of receiving that sacrament, then, if those people will continue to be divided on the most important decisions of their lives? The only logical response is that the decisive importance lies in the vertical and ahistorical – but absolute – importance of the sacrament itself. Needless to say, these remarks about the sacraments could easily be applied to many equally ahistorical features in the Catholic Church and in other Christian denominations: cultic worship, conversion, eschatology, and so forth. Despite theological disagreements about the nature and essence of the sacraments themselves, the use of the sacraments in many Christian churches represents a substitute for the security that should come from our committed efforts to transform and liberate history.

Is it by chance, then, that this conception and practice of the sacraments dovetails perfectly with the interests of the ruling classes and is one of the most powerful ideological factors in maintaining the status quo? Would it be too much to admit the fact that sacramental *theology* has been influenced more by unconscious social pressures than by the gospel message itself?

Irreverent and improbable as the hypothesis may seem, we must realize that at some point in theological tradition an alien element must have been injected into it. Why? Because the Christian sources do not present us with any concept of a religious efficacy that is vertical and ahistorical. In the Letter to the Hebrews, for example, we read: 'He thus annuls the former to establish the latter. And it is by the will of God that we have been consecrated, through the offering of the body of Jesus Christ *once and for all.* . . . For by one offering he has perfected *for all time* those who are thus consecrated' (Heb. 10:9–10, 14).

If someone were to read those lines without knowing the later history of the Church, could he possibly think that the Church would now have religious ceremonies so that human beings might obtain the divine grace they need? Is it not only too clear that if the Christian community is still getting together every week, it certainly is not to fulfill the function that was performed once and for all by Jesus Christ? From the pages of the New Testament itself it is clear that religious efficacy is ruled out for any and every ritual or cultic assembly precisely insofar as the latter is based on the assumption that the grace of God was not given once and for all but must be won and over again in and through such rites.

Ruling out any attempt to take gradual possession of divine grace, Christ freed his Church once and for all so that it could devote itself to its commitment and function in history. But when we note that the overall panorama of the Church presents us with a very different picture, we suddenly realize that someone must hit us over the head with strange-sounding hypotheses so that we may be able to read and interpret even the most clear-cut passages of the Gospels and the New Testament. We must be told that at a certain moment in history the Church stopped listening to the voice of Christ and began to listen to the voice of the ruling classes and their selfish interests. We need these seemingly harmful hypotheses to wake us from our ideological slumber.

It should be obvious to the reader that we have just completed a hermeneutic circle with these remarks on the sacraments. It is a relatively simple thing to do when one is operating out of a commitment to liberation, for one readily suspects that commonly held notions are not as neutral as they are made out to be. Of course the last stage, the new interpretation of Scripture, can call for more than average knowledge of the Scriptures. And one might well debate whether the average Christian should or should not put more effort and energy into learning about the fonts of his faith than into activities that are laden with ideology. Be that as it may, a Church composed of Christians sensitive to reality and Christians more fully acquainted with the sources can and should join together to carry out the task more fully described in the final chapter of this book.

A second example may help us to appreciate this critical task a little more fully. This one has to do with the question of *unity*, to which I have already alluded. The unity in question here is that within a given Christian church on the one hand, and that among all Christian churches on the other. In the latter case we talk about ecumenism.

As Cone made clear in his book, the internal unity of a Christian church can be attained or maintained today only by minimizing and playing down the radical historical oppositions that divide its members. In other words, one must pass over in silence such matters as color, social class, political ideology, the national situation, and the place of the country in the international market. At the same time one must stress the values that are presumably shared by all the members of the Church in question. In short, the Church must pay a high price for unity. I must say that the issues of suffering, violence, injustice, famine, and death are less critical and decisive than religious formulas and rites.

At this point someone might complain, with some reason, that I am erring by going to the opposite extreme; that I am wrong in placing only *religious rites and formulas* over against things that are historically decisive. After all, one might object, don't the shared features go beyond mere formulas and rites? Don't they include a deep faith and general conceptions about God and the importance of eternal life?

If I do not place these latter issues in the balance scale, it is precisely because they are *not* shared in common. Faith in God, for example, is not something shared in common by all. One person pictures a God who allows dehumanization whereas another person rejects such a God and believes only in a God who unceasingly fights against such things. Now those two gods cannot be the same one. So a common faith does not exist within the Church. The only thing shared in common is the formula used to express that faith. And since the formula does not really identify anything, are we not justified in calling it a *hollow* formula vis-à-vis the decisive options of history?

It would seem that the Church cannot arrogate to itself the divine right of choosing between the oppressors and the oppressed precisely because of this overvaluation of Christian unity. For example, on numerous occasions the bishops of Chile have denounced the inhuman consequences of capitalism for the vast majority of Chileans. But when a conflict arose between the capitalist system and a socialist system, they came out and said that the Church could not choose. Why? Because the Church, according to them, belongs to all the people of Chile; to choose one specific option in the name of justice, human rights, or the liberative plan of God, would have excluded some portion of the people from the Church – and therefore from the best opportunities for salvation.

But of course not choosing at certain critical junctures in history is really choosing anyway. If a person or group refuses to choose because they have *higher* values to defend, then they are downgrading the values that are at stake in a given specific situation. They are saying that the latter values are dangerous, inferior, or at the very least secondary. Whether they realize it or not, whether they want to or not, they are thereby helping to perpetuate the existing situation.

Unfortunately this very approach has often been used in efforts to promote unity between different Christian churches. Ecumenism is exalted at the expense of human values. Richard Hofstadter has this pertinent observation on the Catholics of the United States: 'It seems a melancholy irony that a union which the common bonds of Christian fraternity could not achieve has been forged by the ecumenism of hatred ... After more than a century of persecution, it must feel luxurious for Catholics to find their Americanism at last unquestioned, and to be able to join with their former persecutors in common pursuit of a new international, conspiratorial, un-American enemy with a basically foreign allegiance – this time not in Rome but in Moscow.'

The Church responds to such criticisms, of course, alluding to fundamental biblical principles. It points to the 'service of reconciliation' that Christians are supposed to perform, according to Paul (2 Cor. 5.18ff.); it also points to the universal reconciliation that is supposed to come about from Christ's work (Col. 1.20). But in the very process of alluding to these things it forgets that the final eschatological reconciliation mentioned in those very texts is supposed to come to pass in and through the liberation of human beings; that it is not the result of any pious blindness towards existing oppression today and the means to combat it. And one of those means, if not the principal one, is to separate those suffering oppression from those who are its fomentors or accomplices. If such is not the case, then one might ask when did Christ reconcile himself with the Pharisees, or when did Paul reconcile himself with the Judaizers?

The real problem of Christian unity, in my opinion, comes down to this: When will we manage to break that conservative, oppressive, undifferentiated unity of Christians in order to establish an open dialogue with all those, be they Christians or not, who are committed to the historical liberation that should serve as the basis for the 'service of reconciliation' in and through real justice?

Once again, we have made a tiny hermeneutic circle by starting out from common Christian attitudes that are not highly speculative. And it has enabled us to unmask an ideological interpretation of Scripture.

A third and final example is offered us by the notion of *God* which underpins the Church's exaggerated valuation of the sacraments and church unity. If the value of the latter things derives from God, what kind of God are we dealing with? He certainly seems to have a strange conception of human attitudes, and he seems to value them all the more highly when they are separated from any historical commitment.

Before going deeply into this question we would do well to begin by mistrusting the classical formulation of theology. To the extent that academic theology accepts our question at all, it formulates it in the terms we first used at the start of the previous paragraph. It asks: What *notion* or *concept* of God underpins these ecclesial attitudes? But it does not go on to our second formulation of the question: *What kind of God* lies behind such attitudes?

Alfredo Fierro · *Historical-materialist Theology*

Alfredo Fierro, *The Militant Gospel*, Orbis Books, Maryknoll and SCM Press 1977, pp.369–72, 381–82, 386, 398–400, 408–11

All political theology is based on certain presuppositions that have taken on relevance since the appearance of Marx: e.g., the relationship of consciousness (or awareness) to praxis and the determining character of production processes. Most of the time, however, political theology has adopted those presuppositions in a partial and disconnected way at best. Theologians have tended to treat them in a timid and disorderly fashion. The aim of this chapter is to deal with those presuppositions in a methodical and systematic way, thus complementing what is left vague by many theologians. To put it succinctly, we shall adopt Marxism as our hypothesis and then go on to consider what sort of theology is possible on that basis. To do that, one must have recourse to the two ingredients mentioned above. One must consider the expressed or implied rudiments of a Marxist-based theology in the work of recent theologians, and one must also consider the elements provided by the historical-materialist theory itself as expounded by those Marxists who have done their best to grasp Christianity ...

Can there now be a Marxist theology, in the same sense that there has been a Platonic theology and an Aristotelian theology? Egbert Hoeflich answers with a definite yes. With good reason he points out that 'Karl Marx, in his comprehension of reality and truth, is much closer to the Christian faith than was Aristotle.' And he goes on to propose a 'Karl Marx for the church'. His choice of words may not be the most fortunate, since it may conceal a proselytizing intent. It could be used in an effort to baptize Marx and assimilate him to the church, when Marx himself would have forcefully rejected any such effort.

The proposal to fashion a historical-materialist theology is in no way equivalent to an unadmitted effort to Christianize Marx. On the other hand, it does have very much to do with rediscovering the fact that biblical tradition is the most materialistic of all religious traditions, as William Temple pointed out ...

I have already remarked that a theology based on Marxist pre-suppositions in no way purports to baptize Marx, to win him back to the Christian tradition, or to suggest that he is directly beholden to that tradition. This point deserves more extended treatment.

It is not impossible to detect religious factors in the genesis (if not the structure) of Marxist socialism. There is no absence of attempts to adapt Marx *ad usum christianorum*, to see in his work a Judeo-Christian vein, and even to see him as an implicit Christian in the line of the prophets. Sometimes these attempts do proceed from an impartial and objective effort to establish the connections between Marxism and other idea-sets, religious ones in this case; but at other times we find a poorly disguised apologetic and proselytizing attempt to win Marx for Christianity. In the latter instances an effort is made to present Marx as one who continues or reiterates age-old biblical themes. Silenced for many centuries by ecclesiastical tradition, those themes take on new resonance and vitality in the writings of Marx.

Unlike efforts of that sort, a historical-materialist theology leaves Marx's thought alone, accepting all its differences from, and opposition to, Christianity. It does not see Marx as one who picks up and continues age-old themes. Instead it sees him as an original and innovative thinker who proposed new formulations of the issues without worrying about finding any direct analogies with biblical tradition. Historical-materialist theology tries to assume his theory completely in order to see what sort of faith, if any, is possible on that basis.

Concrete elaboration of a historico-materialist interpretation of Christianity in its different phases of development has remained virtually on the rudimentary level provided by Engels. With few exceptions (Bloch, Puente Ojea, for example) today's Marxists have paid no more attention to the history of religion than their predecessors did. There is almost a complete lack of study, from the Marxist and non-Marxist sides, of the material, economic, and social base with which Christian theology was linked at any given moment in history. Such studies could provide us with authentic historical knowledge of the socioeconomic conditionings affecting different past theologies. This in turn would enable us to trace out a social history of dogmatics like that which John D. Bernal has worked out for science and Arnold Hauser for literature and art. The results obtained from such a social history of theology, and only those results, would serve as the touchstone and proof of the historical-materialist hypothesis and its interpretation of the Christian faith.

But the question here is: Is it possible to have a theology that is not conditioned? Of course not. Every theory and every theology has its conditioning factors. One must try to choose them well, to situate oneself in those conditions that will make it possible to formulate a correct theory or theology. In the case of a theology grounded on the hypothesis of historical or dialectical materialism, the sociopolitical condition underlying its feasibility is clear enough: i.e., its effective real-life involvement in the overthrow of social structures based on domination. In the last analysis one is forced to accept the verdict that 'either the theologian is a human being committed to the struggle for liberation or he is not a theologian'.

Why Jesus specifically, and no one else? What is contained in the tradition that derives from him that is not to be found in other religious traditions? Those questions cannot be settled in a dogmatic manner. The correct answer comes in part from history, but mainly from praxis and the future.

For its part, history may be able to show that Jesus possessed an incomparable capacity to stir people to freedom and displayed complete independence vis-à-vis the groups in power. It may even be able to find in him certain qualities that cannot be found to such a high degree in other great religious teachers, who may have been more tied to the ruling ideologies of their day. But even supposing that history could perform this apologetic service, and that is a large supposition, it would only be a partial validation of the Christian option. Complete validation of that option cannot come solely from what Jesus was or said or did; it must also come from the concrete praxis associated with the tradition that goes back to him. The decision to focus on Jesus alone and opt for him is justified insofar as that particular man proves to be capable of generating a liberation praxis that lasts down through the centuries and continues on in the future.

It is Christians working for human liberation who validate and accredit the titles accorded to Christ. It is their praxis that makes Jesus really and truly appear to be the Messiah, the Son of God, the Word made flesh, the ever living one. If people call themselves Christians but foment or accept various forms of human domination over other humans, they make Jesus a liar or a deluder; they make it impossible for anyone to invoke him as the Christ, to derive strength from him. The truth of the belief that Jesus is the Christ finds its verification in the praxis of those human beings who profess fidelity to him. The harsh judgment of Vaccari is correct in the last analysis: 'If man is not liberated, Christ has not risen.'

This attribution of a basic validating function to praxis represents a very definite and concretely verifiable response to a question that has been raised more insistently in recent decades. The question itself has to do with the meaningfulness and validity of religious statements, and it has usually been posed from the standpoint of neo-positivist presuppositions. It has produced theological best-sellers, particularly Van Buren's [*The Secular Meaning of the Gospel*].

A truly satisfactory response to that question, however, cannot be derived from the positivist approach. The question must be explored in historical and dialectical terms. The import and validity of certain beliefs can be seen in the historical consequences that flow from them through the mediating praxis of those who profess those beliefs. A historical-materialist theology sees in this the core of its own grounding and validation. It feels it is solidly grounded when there is an effective praxis that verifies and justifies it. Its pronouncements are true when they are inscribed in concrete praxis. The justification of the Christian faith and its political hermeneutics is to be found in this correspondence of word and deed, of profession and praxis, of symbolic representation and objective social change. The specifically human cast of all things, including faith, emerges from the synchronization of certain activities and certain words. Faith exists as a grounded reality when Christian talk corresponds with Christian praxis, or vice-versa.

There is an idea around today that presents God as the power behind our future and as the only source that can furnish anything really novel to us. This idea, too, is ensnared in the trammels of the older dogmatic view of original sin that sees human beings as incapable of achieving their own nature and humanity without God's intervention. Any such theology is, in the last analysis, caught up in the web of political Augustinianism. According to that conception, human society is incapable of attaining its own ends without the grace of God or the witness of Christians; it can only remain frozen in the old order of things.

The theoretical construct proposed here obviously strips the Christian faith of its unique and singular character. It is not possible to reduce everything to faith or to grace. However much a believer or a theologian one may be, any attempt to reduce history and reality to a theological position is bound to failure, for such a position can never provide a complete explanation. Faith has something to do with everything, but it is not the key to everything. Neither is the material character of production processes the key to everything, though it too has something to do with everything. Our opposition to theological reductionism here is grounded on the very same reasons that dictate our opposition to economic reductionism.

To put it another way, we can say that the theory elaborated here assumes multilateral interaction between varied and diverse human structures. Though it will not be approved by many Marxists and many Christians, it contains nothing that is incompatible with the basic presuppositions of historical materialism on the one hand and the intentions of faith on the other. Only a very shortsighted materialism can ignore the relative autonomy of other realms (the artistic realm, the linguistic realm, the theological realm, and so forth) vis-à-vis the economic base. Only a highly sacral concept of faith can fail to recognize that justice, freedom, and utopia are attainable without having to rely at all on the name of God or on hope in God's advent. Our view here is opposed to both brands of reductionism: that of dogmatic Marxists who see economics as the only key, and that of orthodox theologians who see human beings' relationship to God as the sole key.

Our opposition to these reductionisms is based on a very simple reason: Reductionist thought essentially comes down to a monologue whereas human truth necessarily goes by way of universal consent, which in turn is made possible only by dialogue. Theology, for example, is the discourse of believers and, as such, it is the jargon of a specific concrete group rather than a universal language. But insofar as it aspires to truth, insofar as it aspires to verification, it must become a language of dialogue and communication with those outside the Christian group. This obligation is not always met by various forms of present-day political theology. The language employed by these theologies is often a language closed to any meaningful communication with other human beings and hence inoperative insofar as the future of truth is concerned; it does not allow for any comprehension or understanding of it by non-Christians.

From the standpoint of a critical theology, the truly revolutionary element is not God as such or God's activity but rather the image of God in human beings. Using direct, first-stage theological language, one can say that God liberates us, topples those in power, and guarantees our future. We have noted more than one author doing just that in Part Two of this book. But that is precritical talk. It is like saying that God has brought us a good harvest this year or cured a member of the family. God does not cure, or bring harvests, or liberate, or do battle with potentates. Human experiences and actions such as harvesting, being cured, and winning freedom have experiential elements that are more or less well known; within their own order, however, they do not leave any loophole open for some activity on the part of God.

The real meaning of the assertion that God does something in this order is that some particular image of God is operating in a liberative way to bring about greater justice. This point must be voiced very clearly and insistently on the level of critical theological reflection; otherwise we will fall back into the humbug of *Gott mit uns* or the *gesta Dei per francos*. God is not with the French or the Germans; nor is God with the poor or the oppressed. Indeed there is no certainty that God is with all either. Strictly speaking, God is not with anybody. God does not liberate, or bring peace, or initiate revolutions because God simply does not work in the world. God does not demand justice or prescribe a different society because in reality God does not speak.

Any critical theology must recognize and admit that fact without using evasive language, engaging in a strictly negative theology as it proposes such theses. Once having proposed them, and without denying them in any way, it may be possible to go on to develop a symbolic theology that will concretely specify that negative theology; by talking about the images and symbols of God, rather than about God as such, theology may be able to regain its tongue. But if the language of faith is not to be the delusory projection of vain fantasies, it must go through the dark night and utter silence of a negative theology first.

Operating in the framework of a symbolic theology that has first gone through the rigorous pathway of negativity, we would assign the power of liberating and pacifying and making revolution to the image of God, Christian witness, and the profession of faith. Thus any attempt to expropriate God, to identify God with special interests in society, is strictly and completely ruled out. Theology must be negative and symbolic if it is not to fall back into the old political theology that identified God as such (not God's images) with the empirical reality of society.

Enrique Dussel · *Barbarian Theology*

Enrique Dussel, 'Domination-Liberation: A New Approach' from 'The Mystical and Political Dimension of the Christian Faith', *Concilium*, vol. 6, no. 10, 1974, pp.47–56. Used by permission of The Seabury Press, NY, and Search Press

1. Conditioning of Theological Thinking

It is widely accepted by critical thinkers in Latin America today that all political expansion soon comes to be based on an ontology of domination (an *ad hoc* philosophy or theology). Modern European expansion had as its ontological foundation the *ego cogito* preceded by the actual fact of 'I conquer'. For Spinoza, in his *Ethics*, the *ego* is a fragment of the unique substance of God – a position which the young Schelling and Hegel were to adopt later – the European *ego* had been deified. Fichte shows us that in the 'I am that I am', the 'I' is absolutely fixed. It is an 'I' that is natural, infinite and absolute (and in Hegel definitely divine). In Nietzsche, the 'I' becomes a creative power ('I' as the 'will to power'), while in Hüsserl it becomes the most abstract *ego cogito cogitatum* of phenomenology. The most serious effect is that *the other* or the neighbour (the Indian, the African, the Asian or the woman) is reduced to the level of an idea. The meaning of the other is formulated in terms of the 'I' who dreamed it into existence. The other is made a separate entity, becomes a thing, is abstracted into a *cogitatum*.

Similarly, European theology or the theology of the centre cannot escape from this reduction. The expansion of Latin-German Christianity gave rise to its own theology of conquest. Semitic and Christian thought of the Old and New Testaments was reduced to a process of Indo-European Hellenization from the second century onwards. Medieval European theology was able to justify the feudal world and the *ius dominativum* of the lord over the serf. Tridentine and Protestant theology had nothing to say about the Indian, the African or the Asian (except the Salamanca School and that only for a few decades). Finally the expansion of capitalism and neo-capitalism allowed Christians of the centre to formulate a theology of the *status quo* and the ecumenism of peaceful co-existence between Russia, the United States and Europe so as to dominate the 'periphery' more effectively. The other – the poor – was once again defined in terms of the European 'I': *Ego cogito theologatum*. With the basis of theological thinking so reduced, a parallel reduction occurs in the whole field of theology. Sin is reduced so as to apply only to *intra* national injustice; it is exclusivized, allowed to have no political application, shown to have nothing to do with sex (or at other levels, shown to have an excessive relation to sex). But more seriously the limits and meaning of salvation and redemption are equally reduced to the narrow bounds of the Christian experience of the *centre*. We have an individual salvation, interiorized and other-worldly, resorting frequently to some painful masochistic experience at a given time and place, whereas the true cross of real history demands our life at the least expected moment.

This theology suffers from many unconscious limitations. Firstly, the limitations of the religiosity of German-Latin-Mediterranean Christianity which was accepted without hesitation as real simply because it was Latin. Then there are liturgical limitations, in which the Latin-type liturgy is regarded as the only one acceptable for the Christian religion and which still prevents other cultures having their own liturgies. There are also cultural limitations, in that theology is the province of an intellectual élite, university professors in well-paid and secure posts, a situation far removed from, and unhelpful to the study of Tertullian and St Augustine. There are political limitations, for it is a theology adjusted and compromised by its closeness to the metropolitan power of the world. There are also economic limitations, for this theology finds favour for the most part among upper-class minorities in the bourgeoisie and in the neo-capitalist world (although sometimes there may be poor monks, they belong to 'rich' orders). Finally, there are sexual limitations, because those who think theologically are celibates and have been unable to formulate an authentic theology of sexuality, marriage and the family. For all these reasons, modern European theology from the sixteenth to the twentieth centuries is unconsciously compromised by its connection with the praxis of oppression in the political, educational and sexual fields.

It would be no exaggeration to say that in many respects it is really a theological ideology in that many facets of it remain unseen by virtue of its origins, just as we are unable to see the further side of the moon simply because we are inhabitants of planet earth. And what is still worse, in Latin America there are many progressive theologians who simply repeat the theology of the centre and by so doing they obscure their own message and, to their shame, become just as much advocates of oppression.

2. *Revelation and Faith – the Anthropological Epiphany*

Western theology has for centuries taken certain presuppositions for granted as unquestionably correct. Kant's ontology (which postulates a rational faith), Hegel's (which sees faith as within the bounds of reason) or Heidegger's (the comprehensiveness of Being) admit the Wholeness of being as the only frontier of thought. Being-in-the-world is the fundamental fact, original and primary. Existential theology starts from the basis of the world as the Whole. The fault lies in that, in fact, the Whole is always mine, ours, the European's or the centre's. What passes unnoticed is that I am thereby denying other Christian worlds and other equally valid experiences. I am denying anthropological otherness as a possible starting-point for theological thought.

As the older Schelling so clearly saw in his *Philosophie der*

Offenbarung, faith in the Word of the Other lies beyond ontological reason (the Hegelian *Sein*), an argument that Kierkegaard carried forward (e.g. in the *Postscriptum*). Faith stands upon the revelation of the Other. Revelation is only the out-going message of God, existentially speaking, which sets out the guidelines for interpreting the reality of Christ. In everyday life (existentially), God manifests the hidden secret (the fact of redemption in Christ) by means of an interpreting light (a classicist would put it: *ratio sub qua*), or by supplying guidelines (categories) for all mankind and for all history. God gives not only a specific revelation, but more importantly, the categories which permit us to interpret it. Revelation comes to a peak in Christ with the New Covenant, but it unfolds its potentialities throughout the course of history. What we are trying to stress here is that this revelation is not affected in history by human words alone, but through man himself (as exterior to the flesh or the system), the poor and the Christ-man.

Faith, which accepts the Word of the Other becomes Christian faith when the divine Word in Christ is accepted through the mediation of the poor man in history, who actually lives in a concrete situation. The true showing forth of the Word of God is the word of the poor man who cries 'I hunger'. Only the man who hears the word of the poor (beyond the system, and therefore ana-lectic, which presupposes that he does not believe in the system) can hear it as the Word of God. God is not dead. What has been assassinated is his self-manifestation – the Indian, the African and the Asian – and because of this God cannot reveal himself any more. Abel died in the self-deification of Europe and the centre, and therefore God has hidden his face. The revealed category is clear enough: 'I was hungry and you gave me no food. . . . They also shall ask, Lord, when did we see you hungry?' (Mt. 25. 42–4). Following the death of the 'divine' Europe, there can rise the faith in the poor of the periphery, faith in God as mediated by the poor. The new manifestation of God in history (not a resurrection, for he never died) will be brought about by righteousness and not by endless theological treatises on the death of God.

3. The Praxis of Liberation and Theology

Given the data of revelation and by virtue of living faith, theology is a reflection of reality. Recently there has been much talk of theologies of earthly realities or doubt, leading eventually to a theology of revolution or development. In European circles, to take just the term political theology the matter has sterner implications. But Latin America detects in the theologico-political argument an attempt to restrict the prophetic voice of protest to the narrow national sphere. From this narrow viewpoint the fact of international, imperialist injustice passes unnoticed. But eschatological, undiscriminating protest must reach out not only to the constituent parts of the system, but to the system as a whole.

In the same way the provocative theology of hope betrays the limitations of the critical theory of the Frankfurt School (which influences Metz) and the works of Ernst Bloch (who inspires Moltmann). Both these philosophical hypotheses have failed to overcome ontology and dialectic, and they consider the future as a development of the Self. Although Moltmann understands the future as otherness, he still has difficulty in finding beyond the projection of the system (but this side of the *eschaton*) an historical projection of political, economic, cultural and sexual liberation. Hope extends as far as an historical change in the pattern of life, but not to a radical renewal of the present system with a view to an historical liberation movement as a true sign of eschatological advance. Without this concrete mediation their hopes reaffirm the *status quo* and constitute a false dream.

On the other hand, a European theology of liberation will bring out clearly the question of Christianity and the class struggle, but within the limits of a national Marxism and before moving on to the theory of dependence. It has not yet seen that the struggle of the proletariat within the centre itself, that is, in the metropolitan powers, can be oppressive in terms of the colonial proletariat of the periphery. Classes have been thinking double and may often oppose their own interests at international level. National liberation of the dominated countries goes hand in hand with the social liberation of oppressed classes. Hence the category known as the people takes on a special significance as opposed to the category of class.

Latin American theology derives, by contrast, from the thinking of many politically involved Christians about the praxis for liberating the oppressed. This theology-ethic is a product of the periphery, coming from the outsiders, from the *lumpen* of this world. Their inspiration is not only sheer necessity (the existence within the system of matters needing attention), but also the desire to liberate (Hebrew 'abhôdhāh; Greek – diakonia), that is a ministry of liberation beyond the limits of ontology. And the sphere of liberation is not only political, but also sexual and educational. In fact, this is a theology of the poor, woman as a sexual object and the child.

4. Towards a Theology of Liberation

After the great theology of Christianity from the fourth to the fifteenth centuries and modern European theology from the sixteenth to the twentieth centuries, the theology of liberation of the periphery and of the oppressed is in fact the whole of traditional theology set into redemptive motion from the point of view of the poor. The theology of Christianity (the old model) almost identified the Christian faith with Mediterranean Latin or Byzantine culture, subsequently halting progress. The argument over Latin Vatican II itself is an obvious recent demonstration of this. Modern European theology, individualized and imperialistic, is reproduced in the colonies as progressive theology by those who operate as an oppressive colonial minority and take as the scheme of salvation a theology which for the periphery is meaningless and therefore uncritical. The *status quo* is once again supported. By contrast, the theology of liberation (where a theology of revolution is only a first stage, political theology is just one of the possible applications and the theology of hope looks to the future) is based on the praxis of liberation, or on the movement or way through the desert of human history, moving from sin as the dominating influence exerted by the various systems (political, sexual and educational) to irreversible salvation in Christ and his Kingdom (the *eschaton*). This movement is accomplished by everyman, all people and every age – in short, by the whole of human history. However, there are certain critical periods (*kairos*) in history and Latin America is living through one such period now, when complete eschatological liberation can be more clearly indicated by the prophets, Christians or the Church. Thus the theology of liberation gradually becomes an African or black theology, though to date there has been no response from Asia, and finally a theology of the whole world and of all the oppressed.

The theology of liberation which is coming from Latin American thinkers can be distinguished when its dependence as a theology is realized in the same way as economy or culture is realized to be dependent (the culture of oppression as Salazar Bondy said in Peru in 1968). Gradually this theology discovers its own methods which I have defined as ana-lectic and not only dialectic, in that it is listening to the trans-ontological voice of the other (*ana-*) and is interpreting its message by means of analogies. (The other, however, remains mysteriously distinct from us, until such time as the progress of the movement towards liberation allows us to enter upon its world.) It adds an entirely new dimension to the question of analogies.

For its own part the theology of liberation favours the interpretation of the voice of the oppressed as the basis for its praxis. This is not a private departure within the unified Whole of universal abstract theology, neither is it an equivocal, self-explanatory theology.

Starting from a unique position of diffence, each theologian, and indeed the whole of Latin American theology, takes a fresh look at traditional themes passed down through history, but enters the interpretative process from the distinct emptiness of his new found liberty (that is, with a blank sheet). The theology of a true theologian or a people like the Latin Americans is analogically similar, yet at the same time distinct, and hence unique, original and completely individual. If what is similar becomes univocal, the history of theology will remain European. On the other hand, if difference is made absolute, theologies become equivocal. The aim is not Hegelian identity, nor yet Jasperian equivocation, but analogy. The theology of liberation is a new focus in the history of theology, an analogical focus which has come to the fore after modern developments in Europe, Russia and the United States, and predating to some extent the most recent African and Asian theology. The theology of the poor nations, the theology of world-wide liberation is not easily acceptable to Europeans, who believe too passionately in their own invariable world-wide acceptance. They will not listen to the voice of the other (the barbarians, non-being if we define Being as the European way of thought), the voice of Latin America, the Arab World or South-East Asia and China. The voice of Latin America is no longer a mere echo of European theology. It is a barbarians' theology – as the apologists would say, making the contrast with the 'wise according to this world'. But we know that we have taken up our stand on the further side of the modern oppressive European closed system. Our minds are set upon the liberation of the poor. We point towards the world-man of the future – man who shall be eternally free.

3 · Pentecostal Conscience

In 1941, as the Aryan myth returned Europe to the Dark Ages, Rudolph Bultmann sat at his desk and extolled the virtues of the modern scientific world view. Modern man could no longer believe in spirits and demons. Within twenty years a spirit movement rolled across the world through black Africa, Europe, North America and into Brazil. Within thirty-five years those educated in the modern culture queued to enter cinemas in the hope of being terrified by scenes of spirit-possession and exorcism. All this to the embarrassment of the camp-followers of modern science, though possibly less so to scientists themselves. Nowhere was the embarrassment felt more strongly than in the historical Christian churches, reminiscent only of the dismay with which the Grand Inquisitor received the returned Christ.

So it has always been: the church has indeed been uneasy about the Spirit or the spirits. Indeed this alternative is the root of the problem, for clearly not all manifestations of spirit are Christian or compatible with the Spirit of Christ. 'Now the Spirit expressly says that in later times some will depart from the faith by giving heed to deceitful spirits ...' 'Beloved, do not believe every spirit but test the spirits to see whether they are of God ...' The strange happenings in the early church were not to be ends in themselves: the bizarre was not to be welcomed or fostered for its own sake. For Paul such things could only be countenanced if they were edifying, if they strengthened the faith and the life of the church. 'The fruit of the Spirit is love, joy, peace, patience, kindness, goodness, faithfulness, gentleness, self-control.' And when all is said and done beyond the manifestations there is 'a still more excellent way', which he then describes in the Hymn to Love.

The Spirit of which Paul speaks was experienced first by the church at Pentecost. This was the Greek name for the Jewish Feast of

Weeks, especially the day on which the first fruits of the harvest were offered to the Lord God. For the church it was the first day of the fruits of the Spirit, the outpouring of the Holy Spirit, the Spirit of Christ Jesus. This was not as it would be experienced hereafter, but it was an 'earnest' or 'guarantee', 'the first fruits of the Spirit'. The church saw the manifestations as the fulfilment of the prophecy of Joel that the Spirit would be poured out on the Day of the Lord. The eschatology of the message of Jesus seemed therefore to be confirmed. Their own message about Jesus was therefore to be eschatological. Here were the unmistakable signs of the end of the age, the end of history, the end of the world.

The early church, fervent in the Spirit, expected the End at any time. As the months, years and generations passed the eschatological fervour understandably diminished; curiously, so also did the fervour of the Spirit. It is not possible to account for this fact. Was there a connection between eschatological fervour and receiving the Spirit; was the Hellenistic church more concerned with the assurance which comes from belief than with the assurance which comes from the manifestations of the Spirit; were the new educated leaders too wedded to the rationality of Greek philosophy? Certainly the more institutionalized the church in subsequent centuries the less welcome were the occasional outbursts of the Spirit/spirits. The suspicion with which Paul had viewed such manifestations gradually intensified. The Spirit blows where it wills and can undermine institutions, beliefs, customs and practices. Above all it undermines the authority which otherwise accompanies office and tradition.

Strange, then, that the fervour of the Spirit should be absent from the church through many centuries in which there was a general belief in spirits: stranger still that the revival in the fervour of the Spirit should come in a century which purported to have outgrown such beliefs. Walter Hollenweger, the world authority on the modern Pentecostal movement, maintains that its origins lie in revivalist groups of American negroes. He links this with the emergence of what some sociologists describe as a post-literate culture. Whether blacks at that time were post-literate or still pre-literate their religion was fervent: not primarily related to doctrine or ethics. (Schleiermacher would have approved!) However, another line of development, typified by Edward Irving, is literate and biblical. Irving and others found promises in the New Testament of spiritual gifts which were not evident in the life of the contemporary church. Their fervent prayers for such gifts were answered.

In these two strands we see the seeds of opposition to the historical churches. The Spirit movement is fervent: the institutions mistrust such manifestations and reject the implication that only those baptized of the Spirit are true Christians. The Spirit movement is spontaneous, responsive to the Spirit: the institutions have structures of authority and established procedures for making decisions. In the 1950s, however, the neo-Pentecostal or charismatic movement emerged within the historic churches, most dramatically among Catholics in the United States. This could not have been foreseen, nor the degree of support for it among the bishops. It has even received papal recognition. This new development has gone a long way to overcoming the traditional tension between the movement and the historical churches. As with Paul, the gifts of the Spirit are not seen as an end in themselves but as given for the edification of the church in the service of God.

Most Pentecostalists interpret this in terms of individualistic piety: God's will is that individuals may be saved. They are saved by confessing the Lord Jesus Christ and receiving the baptism of the Spirit. They then glorify God, not least in speaking in tongues.

So it is now, for thus it was at the first Pentecost. Well, yes, but there was also something else at Pentecost. 'And all who believed were together and had all things in common; and they sold their possessions and goods and distributed them to all, as any had need.' There is a constant theme running through the gospels that the followers of Jesus really did not understand what he was about during his ministry. At his arrest they scattered. At his execution they went into hiding. All this was reversed at Easter: the birth of faith, new understanding and courage. Few commentators, however, enquire about their primitive communism. Why was this their response to Pentecost? Was it simply a revival of their experience with Jesus? Or was this their intuitive understanding of the first fruits of the Kingdom? A good deal has been written about the historical Jesus, but this action of the early church must surely throw some light on their new understanding of the message of Jesus. Significantly, it is always ignored.

The fruit of the Spirit, listed by Paul, is largely individualistic, but the early community uncovered cosmic implications. It is the Spirit of reconciliation. Babel is reversed. God and man reconciled, but also man and man. Individuals are saved, but not alone. Individuals enter the New Covenant, but also the new community which experiences now the first fruit of the Kingdom to come. For some, the most exciting feature of the neo-Pentecostal or charismatic movement is the appreciation of this social dimension of salvation and with it the use of the gifts of the Spirit for God's work in the world, to 'let justice roll down like waters, and righteousness like an everflowing stream'. The selections in this chapter give some indication of Pentecostal groups responding to this vocation. Inevitably they will not seem to most readers models which they can readily appropriate. Closer to them is the kind of community formed at the Church of the Redeemer, Houston, Texas. Unfortunately Graham Pulkingham in his account of the development of the community, in *Gathered for Power*, says relatively little about *this* side of the Pentecost experience. It is better described by Michael Harper. A book specifically on this subject would be most helpful. I regard the combination of the prophetic vision and the power of the Spirit as the most dramatic and hopeful development in the church for many centuries.

Carlos Talavera · *Charismatic Renewal and Social Commitment*

Carlos Talavera, 'The Charismatic Renewal and Christian Social Commitment in Latin America Part 1' in *New Covenant* Vol. 6, No. 2, August 1976, pp.4–8. Copyright 1976 by New Covenant Magazine, Ann Arbor, Michigan, USA.

Every commitment we make is social in some sense, even though we may not be aware of it. Therefore, as I write about the charismatic renewal and Christian social commitment, I am not talking about some special new type of commitment. In the final analysis, there is only one: the commitment our eternal Father has to the world. And just as all fatherhood has its origin in the Father of light, so every commitment comes from him who has committed his Son to save the world.

I do not wish to focus on the commitment of the charismatic renewal to social change but on the broader vision of the church's commitment to the world. The church is called to live her ecclesial being to the fullest and, by so doing, to transform the world. The church's main commitment to the world, her true reason for being, is to produce the new creation, renewed in Jesus Christ and enlightened and moved by the Holy Spirit.

I would like to share about two places where this new creation is being manifested: the squatters' camp adjoining Mexico City's international airport, and the municipal garbage dump in Ciudad Juarez, the Mexican city across the border from El Paso, Texas. In both these cities, the Lord is demonstrating his salvation among the poorest, most despised people.

Around Mexico City, squatters are common – poor people who occupy vacant land without legal permission. But the squatters at the airport form the lowest strata of the lowest social class, and are rejected even by fellow squatters. However, in 1972, about two years after the camp first appeared on the airport property, it became the unlikely setting for a spiritual renewal. With Fr Ralph Rogawski and Sr Helen Raycraft, a group from the archdiocesan social secretariat visited the camp and began a charismatic prayer group. The faithful commitment of a factory worker who became the group's leader, Life in the Spirit seminars, and a short course on growth in the Spirit have helped the group to draw together and to grow in conversion and faith. Whenever possible, I celebrate the Eucharist at the camp and so have observed firsthand how wonderfully Jesus has transformed the squatters' lives and relationships.

He is also teaching them to trust him. Two years after the prayer group began, the police came to expel the squatters from their camp. The group immediately joined together in prayer and God gave them his word in Psalm 24: 'To Yahweh belong the earth and all it holds, the world and all who live in it.' That word has sustained the group through all its struggles. Now, not only are the squatters still on the land, but they have been given the legal title to it.

A similar situation has developed among the people who live on the Juarez city dump and scratch out a living by sorting through its garbage for saleable materials. Although a group of social workers was active there for some time nothing of much consequence happened at the dump until some of the workers gave their lives fully to the Lord. One in particular, Guillermina Villarreal de Villalva, began to think of herself less as a social worker than as a herald of the good news. This change in her approach made her more effective and helped trigger other exciting developments.

In 1972, Fr Rick Thomas and other members of a prayer group in El Paso began to consider seriously the injunction in Luke 14: 'When you give a lunch or a dinner, do not ask your friends, brothers, relations, or rich neighbors. . . . But invite the poor, the crippled, the lame, the blind. . . .'

The prayer group decided to respond by sharing a holiday dinner with the poorest people they knew, and so, early Christmas morning, eight carloads of people and food proceeded to the Juarez dump. The Lord blessed their effort and multiplied what they brought; somehow, tamales for 120 people fed almost 300, and there were left-overs.

But more important than the multiplication of food was the Lord's healing work. The people living on the dump resolved their differences and overcame longstanding divisions; they regained a sense of their own personal dignity; their children were healed of many diseases. And like the squatters, the people of Juarez faced and overcame a crisis: in 1975 the manager of the dump refused to pay the workers for the trash they had collected and sorted. Again, the Lord demonstrated his mercy and power. Eventually, the governor turned over the management and income of the city dump to the people who live there.

I am convinced that the Lord wants to use the very poor to teach us how to live more fully in him. There is a lesson for us all in the experiences of the people at the airport and the dump. A closer look at each situation may help underline the point.

Both situations involve people who live on the fringe of society. They have little or no income, no land; most have never finished grade school. Yet, unequipped as they are to enter the mainstream of industrialized civilization, people in both places cherish middle-class aspirations. Unconsciously, perhaps, they have assimilated the values of the rest of society. They want to become rich and increase their possessions – especially those that rank as status symbols.

This mentality among those who live in slum areas reflects the values of other, wealthier sectors of society. The middle and the upper classes are continually absorbing values from other cultures or creating new values based on comfort, luxury, prestige, and power. Their members strive to have the best and to be on top. Economic achievement is prestigious; the ability to realize one's goals, even at the expense of others, is highly esteemed. All the efforts of the lower class are aimed at emulating the upper class. But the values of the residents of the airport camp and the dump began to change. In both places, the Lord began to transform their values from individualism and materialism to mutual help and support.

It is interesting to note a further parallel between the squatters' camp and the dump. In both cases, change was precipitated by members of the middle class. At the archdiocesan social secretariat, I have worked on various projects with groups of middle-class people who were generous and well-meaning and who consistently showed a loving concern for the poor. But for years their efforts yielded only modest results, disproportionate to the heavy personal investment involved.

For middle-class people in Juarez, as well as for us in Mexico City, true conversion – a radical turning to Jesus Christ – has made all the difference. As we have tried to respond to the Lord's call for conversion our middle-class hearts have been changed. The process has required us to lay aside our plans and our way of analyzing society and determining our objectives.

Because we have heard the call for conversion, our prayer groups have concentrated on evangelization. But accompanying this proclamation of the gospel, and considered an integral part of it, we have offered whatever assistance we could. In Juarez this has meant doing administrative work, finding markets, investigating importation procedures. In the squatters' camp the major needs have been legal advice, architectural planning, and financing. Our outside prayer groups have been able to provide these services in a simple, natural manner. After so many years of expensive and highly organized projects with little impact, I can only thank and praise the Lord as I watch him bring forth abundant fruit from our humble efforts.

I want to mention particularly four basic aspects of salvation we have seen God bring about: unity, forgiveness, personal dignity, and a new set of goals.

The sense of unity has its origins in the liberating power of Jesus Christ. Once freed from personal bondage – sins, vices, distorted inclinations, bad family relationships – people can begin to reach out beyond themselves. They can respond to the worth and the needs of others.

I well remember one of the first signs of unity to appear at the squatters' camp. The women gradually banded together to fight a common enemy, hunger. They began to knit and sell clothing. With their small profits, they established a common fund that loans money to the most needy and helps families in emergencies; it has also enabled the group to buy some of their food wholesale, and thus more cheaply. This first experiment has been followed by many other manifestations of unity.

At present, the people in the camp at the airport are sharing Sunday dinner. Because they are convinced that the Lord wants them to spend Sunday praying together – not cooking and worrying about food – the families take turns preparing the meal for everyone. With a little technical advice, the cooks have learned how to serve a well-balanced meal at the low cost of eight cents per person. More tremendous though, has been the sense of oneness resulting from this Sunday project and spilling over into all the other days of the week. Some people, for example, are sharing with everyone the few things in which they had found their security. 'This is no longer mine, this is ours,' they have said of their pigs or chickens. Many have also put their time and talent at the disposal of the community: 'I can lay bricks for you' . . . 'I can sew for you' . . . 'I can cook for you.'

Similar things have happened in Juarez. There, the most immediate and striking sign of unity was the healing of a division between two factions of workers in the dump. After they resolved their differences, they organized their trash industry into a cooperative for which all are responsible and from which all profit.

The unity achieved at the squatters' camp and the dump is not the all-too-familiar, very fragile oneness attained by long, tiring efforts and man-made techinques of social action. On the contrary, the unity in these groups has come about swiftly and powerfully – because it is founded in Jesus Christ. And these initial, concrete signs of oneness are meant to lead – gradually – into a living community.

Forgiveness, the second important aspect of God's salvation in both the squatters' camp and the dump, is one cause of the growth of unity. The Lord means to make his people one, to reconcile them with one another and to obliterate hatred and division. But in order for this to happen, there must exist within the group a continual spirit of pardon, both among its own members and also toward outsiders and members of other social classes.

Forgiveness was obviously important at the Juarez dump, where the Christmas visit quickly stimulated a reconciliation between two bitterly divided groups. Among the people at the airport, too, there has been healing of relationships. Residents of the camp, who at once point were openly hostile to the small prayer group and accused them of 'selling the squatters' interests,' have had a change of heart. They have asked to join the prayer group and have been forgiven and accepted as brothers and sisters.

The squatters also learned how to pardon 'persecutors' from outside their group. For instance, whenever policemen arrived to enforce the rule that prohibits bringing building materials into the camp, the squatters greeted them and tried to serve them. The people in the camp had never smuggled any building materials; they met the suspicions and searches of the police with love.

A similar situation developed with the airport lawyers, who

periodically came to order the squatters off the property, only to be met with coffee, coke, and words of welcome. On one occasion, pained by the realization of their own anger and resentment about the injustices they had suffered, the squatters asked forgiveness of the airport officials.

This spirit of forgiveness has at times evoked some response. An airport lawyer admitted to one woman that he really had no legal ground for evicting the group; and furthermore, he told her, as far as he was concerned, the squatters could remain or leave as they pleased.

All these events serve to underline one truth: continual forgiveness is essential to a truly Christian environment. It is also a key to effective social action.

The third element of salvation which has emerged among the people at the airport and the dump is a strong sense of personal and community dignity. Before their conversion, they tended to consider themselves as without rights or personal value. Their attitude toward civil authorities was marked by exaggerated submission and flattery, as is evident from the pleading phrases of a letter the squatters addressed to the president's wife at the beginning of their struggles. 'I beg you to forgive me for distracting you from your many occupations,' it whimpered: 'I make my plea to you because you have always been so kind to the poor and the helpless.' A more recent letter, however, reflects a change of attitude. While acknowledging that civil authorities have a right and a duty to create and maintain order in society, the authors are equally aware of their own rights and worth as citizens.

This about-face sprang not from pride, but rather from the people's discovery of their true position as children of God. Far from undermining their humility this realization bolstered their sense of personal dignity and replaced their ingrained fear of the 'big, important people.' The residents of the squatters' camp no longer feel intimidated by the presence of members of the middle or upper class. No longer do they feel ashamed of their speech and way of life. Secure in the knowledge that they are children of a loving Father, the people at the airport are now free to approach everyone in a spirit of peace.

I remember what one of the squatters asked me after attending our first national conference on the charismatic renewal. 'Why can't we treat everybody the way we've treated each other these past few days?' he wanted to know. 'I was with rich people, yet I felt close to them – like their brother. There was no such thing as class distinction.'

Another aspect of this growing sense of personal dignity involves the new concept of leadership that is emerging among the squatters. Instead of the traditional approach – one person rises up as the leader who 'handles all the problems' – the prayer group exercises authority on a community basis. After prayer, the group decides which member should handle a specific situation; the group does not always choose the same people. Besides serving as a safeguard against the corruption that often results from one-man rule, this system of group leadership reinforces everyone's sense of dignity. It elicits qualities of responsibility, personal freedom, leadership, and creativity from many, not from just a few.

The group is finding new ways of doing things, new solutions to their problems. Their most notable proposal to date involves housing; the homes they plan to construct soon will be owned by the community, rather than by individuals. Even the government has expressed interest in the project. Not only is it free of any 'leader' who stands to make a profit, but it represents a new life style that could be of help to many other communities.

Fourthly, God's power at work among the poor has effected a profound change in their goals and ideals. Formerly, the objectives of the squatters and dump dwellers were pretty much limited to the legitimate desires of members of all social classes. A survey of the residents of the airport camp showed them anxious to repair their houses, pay their debts, improve their nutrition, and educate their children. And yet all of these natural, important goals have been overshadowed by a higher one, as illustrated by the following incident.

At one point during their struggle for land, the squatters were offered space in two housing areas in different parts of the city. One was a high rise apartment building, the other was a group of small houses on common farm land, but neither place fitted the needs of the group as a whole. The squatters visited both, then returned, prayed, and decided not to move. Later, they explained their decision to me: 'That farm was such a pretty little place. But you see, we are sure the Lord wants us all together.' Only Jesus, I concluded, could have brough them to such a realization. Only he could have led them to put community goals over individual ones, to forego comfortable living quarters in order to share their life together as one Body in him.

A few months ago, there arose a further proof that this community interest is stronger than the desire for private property. Instead of following the usual procedure and slicing up the land accorded them by the government, the people at the airport camp decided against individual ownership. While providing for some privacy in their sleeping and living quarters, they chose to keep some facilities in common: the dining room, kitchen, garden, recreation center, and community center for children, and some workshops. Because this plan deviates from the usual laws of property ownership, it has delayed the legalization of the deeds. The residents, however, consider their plan worth waiting for.

Their fundamental change in goals has affected the poor people's attitude toward hand-outs. Rare are hungry and homeless people who are not eager to receive something for nothing; the squatters were no exception. Now, however, they refuse hand-outs. They have learned that it is harmful for their children to become passive receivers.

They have also understood the importance of sharing with others what they themselves have found: God's own life, and a strong sense of community. The people at the airport have returned to the high-rise apartment buildings – not to live there, but to form prayer groups among the residents.

Unity, forgiveness, an awareness of personal dignity, and a change in goals – these are flowers blooming in the slums. To me, they are lessons in the power of God's salvation. Our prayer groups, our church, can learn from what the Lord is doing among his faithful poor.

Arthur M. Brazier · *Black Self-determination*

Arthur M. Brazier, *Black Self-determination*, W. B. Eerdmans, Grand Rapids 1969, pp. 5–6, 23–26, 30

The message of this book is simple. Black Americans must enter the mainstream of American life now. The nation must choose between democracy and repression, between the republic and a police state; for America cannot keep down thirty million people who are moving up, without destroying the entire nation in the process.

In order to enter the mainstream, black Americans must acquire power through organization. They must organize for their basic self-interests. They must organize in order to find their own identity, dignity, and destiny. They must organize to keep from being exploited or helped in paternalistic ways by white society. Only then will people of color be powerful enough to claim a rightful place in American life.

When black people organize, white people panic and strike back. White society will not relinquish the power with which it has held the black man in his 'place' for almost four hundred years – not without fighting every step of the way. History has shown that black people cannot rely on the moral integrity of organized white society to give power to black people voluntarily. It must be wrested from that society. The price of acquiring power is conflict and confrontation; but neither need be violent. Black Americans must seize the right and power of self-determination now.

There are two facets to this problem. Black people need a way out of the ghetto into an open society in which they can freely move, and they need control over their life situation within their community wherever they are.

Black people must reject everything negative the white man has said about them. Every sign and hint of racial superiority in the thinking of whites must be denounced by blacks. White men dragged the black man to this country against his will, stripped him of his African heritage, gave him a nondescript name, called him a Negro instead of an African, called him a boy instead of a man, rejected his racial characteristics, imposed a servile personality on him, and coerced him into believing he was inferior. Blacks cannot allow this fantastic myth of white superiority to influence them any longer. They must identify with blackness, see that black is good, generate pride in religion, culture, family, race. People of color need not prove their equality at the bar of white justice; they can claim it as a historical fact.

The time is here for black people in America to organize the black community from within for self-determination. Without this organizing and the power that grows from it the black man will not be able to enter the mainstream. The black community at the present time faces two problems with organization. It is organized from the outside by white society for the political and economic interest of whites. It is splintered from within by a multitude of organizations that have only fragmentary influence but no real power. Black men must make united, organized efforts to deal with every facet of their own interests in the face of resistance from the Establishment outside and from narrow divisive forces inside.

A myriad of local groups take the first step toward organization, and then get bogged down in their own inertia. A total organization must be set in motion having the strength to go on to take the second, the fifth, the twentieth step. This book is largely about how one black community took such steps and what it is doing for the future.

In this the church has a role to play. The church led the way in understanding and implementing the struggle of the black man for identity, dignity, and self-determination in Woodlawn. Withdrawal of the church into a purely spiritual ministry is indefensible, especially from a biblical Christian view. To do nothing is to take sides with the Establishment in maintaining the oppressive status quo against the black community. By positively affirming the rights and the gifts of the black man and by helping him to take effective action, the church can underscore the preaching of the gospel of salvation in Christ by responsible living in Christ.

Woodlawn distrusted and feared white society. The fear of the white suburban man for the black ghetto cannot compare with the fear the ghetto dweller has for the white suburbs. The exploited and fearful people of Woodlawn did not appear on the surface to have the kind of stuff it takes to do such things as forcing the University of Chicago to come to terms with them on urban renewal, grappling with Mayor Daley on issues ranging from intolerable housing to inadequate schools, standing off the police, cleaning up unscrupulous business practices of some of Woodlawn's merchants, negotiating a million-dollar youth training program with the Office of Economic Opportunity, working with its own 'gangs' in sponsoring and operating the program, and participating as an equal partner with the public schools of Chicago and the University of Chicago on an experimental school district.

Precisely these things happened on the south side of Chicago in the decade of the sixties. They came about through organization – The Woodlawn Organization. They happened because people in Woodlawn developed a near obsession for self-determination. They came about because the church cared and risked its reputation to step out and initiate action. They happened because some liberal subsystems of the establishment supported what was happening in Woodlawn. The Woodlawn Organization was not without its failures – failures that hurt but did not crush the organization.

How did all this come about? We look back a decade to where it started.

Four pastors in the community were deeply concerned about the conditions of Woodlawn in the late fifties. Their many conversations continually came back to a basic inescapable conclusion that within two or three years Woodlawn would become a major slum unless a vigorous community organization was developed to stem the deterioration that was spreading across the community. Sensing that they would need help from the outside they agreed together that each would take the initiative in conferring with leaders of their respective church organizations for this help.

At the request of the four pastors the national leaders of the churches to which they belonged met early in 1959 to consider the pastors' analysis of the desperate situation in Woodlawn. The pastors presented as an imperative that the national organizations of the churches support the efforts of the local congregations in organizing the community. The church leaders agreed that continued conversation and planning should be undertaken. The four pastors in the community drew up a document outlining the basic needs of the community as a first step.

The leaders took a second important step. The members of the Roman Catholic Church suggested that the Woodlawn community needed a powerful, hard-hitting community organizing program similar to that accomplished some years previously in the formation of the Back-of-the-Yards Council, by the Industrial Areas Foundation. The IAF, a controversial organization headed by Saul Alinsky, provides technical services to communities who want to organize themselves. This suggestion was taken seriously, and after a great deal of controversy the community turned to IAF for help.

As a third step the representatives of the Catholic Church offered to secure a $50,000 grant from Catholic sources to start such an organizational program if the Presbyterians and Lutherans would each contribute a similar amount. This financing, supplemented by available foundation grants, would provide a sufficient basis for the first three years of work. Representatives of the churches felt that at the end of three years the residents and institutions of the community would be fully ready to finance the lower cost of continuing a community-wide organization.

In April 1959, upon the recommendation of the church leaders the four pastors from Woodlawn drew up a document entitled *The Woodlawn Cooperative Project*, in which they stated:

> For more than a year the pastors of the Holy Cross Catholic Church, The Woodlawn Emmanuel Lutheran Church, and the First Presbyterian Church of Chicago consulted with each other in

regard to the tragic problems of social and physical deterioration of the Woodlawn community. In the process of attending meetings of various community and civic organizations, by participating in the activity and programs of these Woodlawn groups, by conversing with residents and block clubs, and by consulting widely with officials of other governmental, educational and religious organizations related to Woodlawn, these pastors found that 1) the Woodlawn community as a whole was not represented by any one organization: 2) that blight, over-crowding of residential buildings, transiency, crime and social disorganization was dangerously on the increase; 3) that this community deterioration began slowly during the depression of the thirties and was sharply accelerated by the housing shortage during World War II and was intensified by postwar inflation coupled with rent control; 4) that racial change in the community began around 1949 and 1950 and within six years the population became some 90 percent non-white. The first Negro residents were well-to-do, stable families seeking relief from the intolerable housing and social conditions of the ghetto further north and west. The same exploitive forces which plagued the Negro residents in Chicago for many years again capitalized on the racial change in the Woodlawn community in the following ways.

(*a*) Property acquisition through scare tactics, and panic selling.

(*b*) Conversion of larger apartments into smaller, cheaper quarters for a more transient and socially unstable population.

(*c*) Development of furnished kitchenette units in apartment hotels catering to all kinds of temporary and irresponsible occupants.

(*d*) Increase in tavern activity coupled with the influx of dope peddlers, prostitutes, and gambling interests.

The document went on to say that those who had sought to give leadership to the community had continually been divided against one another in a variety of personality, policy and organizational conflicts. Even the Woodlawn Ministers' Alliance had become inactive because of the division of loyalty among various community action groups and the general discouragement with the chaotic leadership pattern in the area. This document established firmly the need for the churches to become actively involved in improving the quality of living in the Woodlawn community.

It is significant that the religious leaders of Woodlawn and not the political or business leaders first saw the need for a strong organization in the community. Many people believe the pastor should limit his activities to Sunday morning sermons, counseling those of his parishioners who are having difficulties, and visiting the sick. The Greater Woodlawn Pastors' Alliance, however, felt that while ministers should continue to function in their traditional role they should not close their eyes to the very real suffering and human misery caused by the exploitative forces in the community. An early draft of the constitution and by-laws of the Greater Woodlawn Pastors' Alliance stated, 'This Alliance is based upon the belief that a community's religious institutions can and must make a contribution to the general welfare of the people that transcends the ordinary concerns of the church.'

So The Woodlawn Organization was born. Power was being generated and organized in the Woodlawn area. A people-oriented organization from its very inception, TWO had the support also of most of the churches in the community. It had the consulting service and staff provided by the Industrial Areas Foundation. The following chapters tell of the struggles, triumphs, and frustrations of The Woodlawn Organization.

Walter J. Hollenweger · *A Pentecostal Co-operative*

Walter J. Hollenweger, *Pentecost Between Black and White*, Christian Journals Ltd, Belfast 1974, pp.42–49

'The Mesquital region of the state of Hidalgo in Mexico is one of the driest and poorest places of the country. Prairie-like valleys are framed by yellow mountains. During the day the sun burns mercilessly and at night it can become very cold, as the valleys are 6,000 feet above sea-level.' (Tschuy).

Industrialization which invaded Mexico City, Monterrey and Guadalajara in the fifties, had not yet reached the region of Mesquital, where agriculture and a small cottage industry give a very meagre income and where in 1960 more than half of the population still spoke the Indian Otomi language. Those Indians can again be divided into half who speak Otomi exclusively and those who, beside their Indian language, have mastered some Spanish. More than a third are illiterate.

The results of the political and social revolution, which conquered the big cities between 1910 and 1917, reached the country of the Otomi much later. Far into the thirties one could find hardly any Protestants here. Those who dared to confess the new faith were either driven away or killed.

That is why in 1936 a young Indian by the name of Venancio Hernandez had to leave his native valley and the hacienda where he and his ancestors had worked since the arrival of the Spaniards. After having taught himself to read and write, he managed somehow to get hold of a Bible. He began to read it, at first very sceptically because he knew that the great Mexican revolution was very consciously anti-ecclesiastical if not anti-religious. As an Indian he knew too how the religion of the conquerors had been thrust on the native population often by brute force and how the hierarchy of the church sided at the time of the war of independence at the beginning of the nineteenth century with the Spaniards and the foreign king.

Yet the Bible which Venancio Hernandez now read appeared to him to be entirely different. The Christ which it described was not half hidden by the Virgin Mary or the Saints. He was neither a poor and feeble child nor a thorn-crowned, weeping, dying or even dead son of God. On the contrary: he spoke with authority, he showed courage, he did not fear the mighty ones of this world nor the indignation of the people who had expected another Messiah. Such a personality would have fitted the Mexican revolution well! More: this Christ talked with individual people about their sin, their *lostness*, about the revelation of God through this Christ, on his love for man, on his sacrificial death, by which he reconciled man with God. One only had to accept this gift ...! Why had somebody never brought such a message to Venancio Hernandez? The Virgin Mary, the Saints, the places of pilgrimage and the indulgences: all this was not at all necessary if that book were true. And it was true, for he acquired an inner confidence which had been unknown to him hitherto. Here was a message which finally gave the right spiritual guidance to his revolutionary thinking and his search for social and political justice.

Venancio Hernandez did not want to and could not remain silent. During the siesta he read to the other farm workers from the wonderful book. They believed and were converted, changed their old habits and all of a sudden, under a tree, where they assembled, the listeners were transformed into a small congregation.

The owner of the hacienda was informed that some of his

Indian farm workers had become Protestants. He summoned Venancio Hernandez and his friends before him and prohibited them to have any further religious meetings. The Indians did not answer. But common prayer and Bible reading went on. The owner of the hacienda, the local priest and other Indians agreed on driving out the small congregation from their valley under threat of death.

Under the leadership of Venancio they wandered across into the next valley to the village of Ixmiquilpan where the main road from Mexico City to Guadalajara passes. Outside the village, on a little hill on which the army had installed a small observation post, the small group settled down taking advantage of the military post which gave them a certain protection. Hernandez knew that the small congregation had to stick together if it were not to risk its sudden death. It was at this time that the system of land reform limited estate ownership to at the most five hundred hectares. That is why one of the big land owners of Ixmiquilpan had to sell part of his land. Venancio and his followers approached him and managed to get a favourable contract. They bought a good piece of land with irrigation rights. As they possessed very little cash, the former owner allowed them to repay the amount of the purchase price by instalments. The small evangelical community of Christians had impressed him and, in spite of pressure from other quarters, he gave them a chance. 'God has been with us!' said Venancio ponderingly when recalling those pioneer days.

The newly acquired farm land was under collective ownership, but the land on which the small stone houses were now gradually being built and the family gardens were privately owned – up to this time the Indians had lived only in Cactus huts. They organized themselves in agricultural co-operatives and built a co-operative textile factory which they continue to modernize. Compared with technical advances in Europe and America their tools and machines are modest. Yet the outstanding fact is that the Indians have created it themselves. Therefore they are not dependent on foreign finance and expertise – even in the form of missionaries – for this handicraft production fits in with their tradition. However it has to be admitted that these Indians are unusually gifted both intellectually and manually. With precision and expertise such an Indian will install a projector together with a generator (in order to produce the necessary electricity) and will not forget to check all the contacts carefully. He is also able to service and repair his versatile agricultural tractor himself.

Their church had to undergo heavy persecutions years ago from the local Catholic clergy. 'Sometimes the priest said that we were not good people, even that we were of the devil', they recalled later to Maria Amerlinck who made a careful anthropological study of the Pentecostal church at Ixmiquilpan. 'In fact', Maria Amerlinck comments, 'persecution had not been initiated by the priests, but by some of the richer people of Ixmiquilpan who could count on the local political structure and who disliked the acquiring of land by the Indians. Yet with the help of regional and national political forces and with some economic help from outside the difficulties were overcome.' Pentecostals considered it to be their duty not to respond to persecution with vengeance. 'By praying and reading the Bible they searched for the will of God and instead of exercising vengeance they offered pardon. The murderers recognized their wickedness, repented and became members of the church.' (Tschuy).

When the governor of their state needed workers for building roads, they make the following offer: 'We know', they said, 'that you want to build roads in our region but that you lack workers. We will provide three hundred men daily free of charge if you provide machines and technical know-how. That is how we are going to show to you that we "cristianos" are useful citizens.' By this demonstration they were able to prove better than by a theoretical statement that they were not – as their persecutors affirmed – sectarian, but responsible members of society. During the road-building they composed new songs in the soft restrained style of the Otomi. Today these songs form part of their liturgy and remind them of the time of persecution and how it was overcome.

The church is no longer threatened by the Catholics. Indeed the latter are ready to learn from Venancio who has, for example, been made a member of the Advisory Theological Commission of the Catholic Church of Mexico. Today the church is threatened by a different 'true faith'. I was personally present at a service in Ixmiquilpan at which an American missionary was the preacher. At the beginning of the service three young Indians came forward with their guitars, knelt down and quietly prayed. Then they played and sang with a cultured restraint and manner which was extremely moving. Even the members of the congregation did not sing at the top of their voices, as one usually finds in Pentecostal circles. But then came the missionary's sermon! His words went back and forth across the Indian congregation like a steamroller. The Indians gently lowered their heads but even so I thought it scarcely possible for them to sustain this flood of oratory without injury. But four centuries have developed in them a capacity to remain dignified and noble even in humiliation. When the appeal for conversion was issued, many of them came to the front, covered their face with their *rebozos* and quietly wept. Before the end of the service the missionary and his entourage quit the chapel. In the house of the chief a large table was spread with a dozen varied Mexican dishes, lovingly and skilfully prepared, together with native fruits and drinks. The missionary talked incessantly – in English, which the Otomi do not understand – while the chief stood at the door with his wife and served the guests. When the food had disappeared, everyone rose. 'Excuse me,' said the Indian chief, 'I have a sick friend and I would like you to pray for him.' 'Of course', answered the missionary, 'Let us pray.' And in his booming voice he rattled off a prayer: 'Lord, You can heal even from afar. Make our unfortunate friend well. Amen. But now we have to be going.' And with that, he went. But Venancio was sorry for him. How could the missionary be blamed for being a *gringo*!

The secret of Venancio's congregation lies in its theological and economic independence. I cannot find out exactly when Venancio united his congregation with the Iglesia Cristiana Independiente Pentecostés whose headquarters are in the nearby Pachuco. He is head pastor and has under him about forty *obreros*, lay preachers who in addition to their work as farmers and craftsmen serve about forty congregations each numbering about a hundred.

The upward social movement of the members of the church is phenomenal. 'There is a close link between evangelism and the search for education', says Maria Amerlinck, a Catholic anthropologist. Giving their testimony, participating in the life of the congregation, financing the church themselves, 'develops' the gifts which are latent in these Indians to their full potential. For them 'giving' (money, animals, vegetables, even drinks) to the church is not 'alms-giving', because God is not a beggar (*limosnero*). She sums up her assessment as follows: 'Under these circumstances religious conversion is the only way out of the narrow confines of traditionalism ... The Indians need this new ideology as a means of rationalization which enables them to understand their relationship to the changing world around them and gives a definite dignity to the individual person.'

While in the Catholic church in Ixmiquilpan most of the priests are foreigners, the Pentecostals have exclusively native ministers (who almost without exception earn their living in secular work). Before their conversion most of them were employed as farm workers on a day-to-day basis. Today most of them are farm-owners, masons, owners of small shops and mills, lorry drivers and mechanics.

The Pentecostal pastors do not consider their ministry as a purely religious ministry which would distinguish and separate them from the rest of the population. They do not see themselves as paid specialists of religion, but very much more as 'economic evangelists' of a kind, or 'evangelistic development advisers'. They earn their own living because their example and the way in which they build their own houses (many of them are masons!) is part of their proclamation. They feel themselves to be superior to the Catholic priests and are very proud of their special ministry of evangelism. They criticize the priests openly – and, if opportunity arises, also the Catholic hierarchy – because they work solely as priests and lay themselves open to the reproach that they exercise their ministry for money. Discussing the question of a full-time and paid ministry, they said: 'What would our colleagues at work say? As a full-time ministry we would become estranged from them.' Hernandez resumes the theology of their *lived fellowship* in these words: 'The community believes in the salvation of the hands by work, of the mind by learning to read, of the body by divine healing and of the soul by new birth.' (Tschuy).

There is no doubt that the Otomi have created an example of development policy which by its very simplicity is fascinating. In this they have explicitly included the women – a revolutionary act in their society. Here and there, but very reluctantly, there are the beginnings of a dialogue with European theology and churches (Niemoeller). The attempt is not without dangers. Maria Amerlinck draws attention to the growing paternalism, particularly by the leaders in Pachuco. Their theological and economic independence is impressive and was a matter of life and death in the pioneering phase of the church. But will it last in the more complex economic situation of the future? And what will the Otomi do if they are restricted by political and economic power structures which cannot be overcome easily by their methods of self-help?

It is also possible that in a wider sphere the intelligence, the charm and the theological understanding of the Indians will produce a solution which we Europeans have not discovered yet. But in order to give any solution the necessary scope, their buried humanity and culture must be excavated in a broader, in an ecumenical, field.

4 · Feminist Perspectives

In *A Reader in Political Theology* I wrote confidently about black theology in the United States and South Africa and about liberation theology in Latin America. It was understood that since I am a European I do not write as a black or as someone from the Third World. Nor does this mean that I am disqualified from making any comment. I take it that the same is true of this present chapter on 'Feminist Perspectives'. The parallel is not without significance since there are similarities among the movements for liberation in the Third World, Black Consciousness and the Women's Movement. In all the diversities of human cultures a common feature has been the oppression of women as women. Indeed even liberation movements have not always included among their goals the liberation of women. A good example of this is to be found in the emancipation of blacks in the United States at the time of the Civil War. Women came to realize that they could not rely on gaining rights by associating with any other movement. The Women's Movement is sometimes dated from the Seneca Falls Convention on Women's Rights held in 1848.

In recent years we have become aware of innumerable minority groups seeking rights. The Women's Movement would be significant if only because it concerns more than half the world's population. It is potentially the most important development in human history, representing as it does a particular rejection of the merely biological and a conscious affirmation of precisely that which leads to the emergence of the human and humane. It has certainly been a long time in coming and it can only be described as a movement, not an event. The wider its influence the greater its effect: it could well influence the course of world history. When linked to the ecological crisis (see chapter 8) it could contribute significantly to the possibility of continuing life on this planet.

All of these superlatives I believe to be quite justified, but whether the potential will be actualized is another matter, and this does not depend solely on the response of men. Some of the most strident critics of the movement have been women: this is to be expected. The most bitter attacks on trade union leaders often come from the shop floor: peasants were a greater problem than the Czar in the formation of the USSR. The opposition to the Women's Movement has not always been from men. To the contrary, Lenin wrote from Zürich in 1917: 'If women are not drawn into public service, into the militia, into political life, if women are not torn out of their stupefying house and kitchen environment, it will be impossible to guarantee real freedom, it will be impossible to build even democracy, let alone socialism.'

Although the movement has a long history it came to prominence in the 1960s especially in the terrifying tones of American middle-class women. It was a decade of liberation movements and the Women's movement unfortunately was tempted to the rhetoric of the day. Some minority movements simply wanted a slice of the action and far from challenging the action hoped that it would continue till they got in on it. This can be seen in the development of black capitalism and in some instances black facism. The state recognized such attitudes and knew perfectly well how to deal with them. They posed no real threat to the existing arrangement of things, exhibited no potential. The women's lib. phase was therefore a cul de sac, for it demanded for women what men claimed for themselves. Or rather it preserved, with a nod and a wink, the structures of injustice and oppression but made room for a few women who by education and training did not represent women in general and could not be taken as signs of hope for women at large. The lasting contribution of the liberation phase may have been a vague feeling among women that there must be something better than being oppressed by men or trying to beat them at their own game. What is to be gained by a reversal of roles? 'This morning, like any morning, I awoke at the first sound of the children squabbling, and got up to make the family breakfast. She was still lying there, snoring with her mouth open, taking up two thirds of the bed with her great, sprawling feminine limbs ... As usual too, the boys had made their beds and folded their night-clothes and were already setting the table. My daughter, of course, had wet her bed, kicked her football through the transom, and was insisting on eating her cereal with boxing gloves on.' So runs Alan Brien's 'Diary of a Martian Male' (*New Statesman* 1971). It may bring a smile and a twinge of conscience but it also underlines the fact that there is no progress while the sexes are still at war.

Fortunately the movement has turned to another path and as the Feminist Movement it is engaged in a much longer haul but one which may yet liberate both oppressed and oppressors. It has also turned away from an earlier Manichaeism (in common with the Black Liberation Movement) in which all virtue and good sense were claimed for women, all vices and stupidity laid at the door of men. Another indication of maturity is a willingness to hear comment or criticism and judge it on its merits. In many Western countries there is now legislation prohibiting sex discrimination over a wide range of jobs or activities. It is easy to underestimate the power of legislation in the changing of attitudes. Reinhold Neibuhr pointed to the effect on American whites of having to serve in integrated units during the Second World War. But more important is the change of climate in which such legislation is enacted. The onus is now on those who discriminate to show cause. In this respect the church has once again fallen behind new and widely shared social standards. Or rather some churches. The Church of Scotland ordains suitably qualified candidates, whether male or female. The Church of England does not at the moment judge that women candidates are suitable.

Most writing on the subject has naturally been concerned with the attitude of the Catholic hierarchy. Mary Daly reports that in 1966 two women correspondents were turned away from a ceremony in the Sistine chapel. An Italian bishop explained: 'This is for the Pope a special day. We must not allow a woman to sully the Sistine Chapel for His Holiness.' In 1972 the Pope told a national conference of Italian Catholic Jurists that the true liberation of women lay in their vocation to be mothers. The attitude persists. Unfortunately the debate or confrontation has focussed on the question of ordination of women. But this is to obscure the matter and return to the old liberationist stance. Women might make more of a contribution by asking why the hierarchy are ordaining *men* to the priesthood. Only when the inherent problems about ordination are resolved will it be clearer whether women might want to serve God in this way.

This example points to a contribution that the Feminist Movement is in danger of failing to make. I have read black theology in the hope of having pointed out to me how traditional theology has been largely an expression of white values and interests. But I find the contribution of the black perspective minimal. Similarly I hope in reading Latin American theology to gain perspective on European theology. This has been more fruitful. Similarly I hope that feminist theology will uncover elements in theology which simply reflect male prejudices. Feminist theology might then make a contribution to theology. I do not think feminist theology can be an end in itself. But there is a danger that feminist theologians will take on board the agenda of a tradition dominated by men. They will not make their most important contribution till they are able to revise the agenda. Otherwise they will simply be encapsulated in the existing framework. They will get on the conference circuit under the Dr Johnson principle: not that they do it well, but that they do theology at all.

Mary Daly · *The End of the Looking Glass War*

Mary Daly, *Beyond God the Father*, Beacon Press, Boston 1973, pp.184–85, 189, 189–90, 193–98. Copyright © 1973 by Mary Daly. Used by permission of Beacon Press.

We might consider the probability that if the male intellectual elite has been fixated upon a split between becoming and being, this in all likelihood reflects the situation of the elite, who benefit from a static, hierarchical cultural climate and who would be threatened by total openness to the future. 'Becoming' then becomes domesticated under the reign of reified 'being,' which can represent 'things as they are' to the consciousness of the privileged who want it that way. It would not serve such interests if 'becoming' were to blow off the lid of objectified 'being.' Marxist criticism of Christian hierarchalism and oppressiveness, while it wasn't deep enough, did manage (along with other influences) to generate a frantic scurry among theologians to leap on the bandwagon of futurism and find a scapegoat for the disease of Christianity. Having managed to blame 'the Hellenic influence' for Christian servility to oppressive powers, they now offer us the 'future' of incorporation with Yahweh & Son. Women who have finally come to recognize that we are *per definitionem* excluded from management in that 'corporation' can recognize here a continued hardening of the arteries that should link 'being' and 'becoming.' The institutional fathers are still running the show In the Name of the 'Future,' which is another word for past.

Bachofen pointed out that the patriarchal principle is one of restrictions and that after the crushing of the original matriarchy, which was characterized by openness to others, the principle of hierarchy took over. I am adding that as long as this system prevails, human becoming is held down by objectified 'being,' which is the demonic distortion of Be-ing. Women have the power to open the channel so that being and becoming find their essential unity. We can do this by be-ing. But time is short. The senior and junior executives of the secular coporations that are the natural offspring and allies of Yahweh & Son are already programming us out of any significant role in the future. The gynocidal-and-therefore-genocidal mania of the patriarchs has already been transferred to The Holy Father Computer, who is heir to the papal throne of a secular Christendom that wills to devour the world. The Corporation of God the Father has formed a merger with the Earthly Town Fathers on the sly (soon to be subject to an antitrust suit). Together they have sent nocturnal emissions beyond the earth's atmosphere, bringing forth signs and wonders in the heavens, converting nearby outer space into a celestial junk yard. The Kingdom of Heaven, then, is at hand. Before it is too late, let it be said that Heaven is not a Kingdom. Let it be spoken by the word of our lives.

There is a seductiveness about philosophies (even more than in the case of theologies) which use language that is not totally distorting, but which do not explicitly move out of patriarchal space. The fact that philosophers of the future do not speak directly to the problem of sexism is a warning. 'Whiteheadians' can be oblivious to the 'process' of the female half of the species in our struggle to become. The essential thing is to hear our *own* words, always giving prior attention to our *own* experience, never letting prefabricated theory have *authority* over us. Then we can be free to listen to the old philosophical language (and all philosophy that does not explicitly repudiate sexism is old, no matter how novel it may seem). If some of this language, when heard in the context of female becoming, is still worth hearing, we need not close our ears. But if we choose to speak the same sounds they will be formally and existentially new words, for the new context constitutes them as such. Our process is *our* process.

But if we perceive the good, the final cause, as *not* identical with the static, timeless being of Parmenides, and *not* identical with the intentions of the institutional fathers and their Heavenly Father, but rather with Be-ing in which we participate actively by the qualitative leap of courage in the face of patriarchy, the magic collar that was choking us is shattered.

The circle of eternal return that neutralized the implicit futurism in Greek thought and that constitutes the alleged futurism of Christian symbols can be broken if women break the chain of nonbeing by be-ing. In this sense, our cause can function as 'the final cause,' that is, by incarnating the desire to break out of the circle and communicating that desire, awakening women and consequently men to become ourselves. The final cause is the beginning, not the end, of becoming. It is the first cause, giving the motivation to act. The feminist movement is potentially the source of real movement in the other revolutionary movements (such as Black Liberation and the Peace Movement), for it is the catalyst that enables women and men to break out of the prison of self-destructive dichotomies perpetuated by the institutional fathers. Radical feminism can accomplish this breakthrough precisely because it gives rise to an intuition of androgynous existence. Only radical feminism can act as 'the final cause,' because of all revolutionary causes it alone opens up human consciousness adequately to the desire for nonhierarchical, non-oppressive society, revealing sexism as the basic model and source of oppression. Without the power of this vision to attract women and men so that we can will to transcend the whole array of false dualisms, there will be no real change. The liberation 'movements' that leave sexism unchallenged can, of themselves, only spin delusions of progress, bringing about endless, arbitrary variation within the same senescent system.

It requires a kick in the imagination, a wrenching of tired words, to realize that feminism is the final and therefore the first cause, and that *this* movement *is* movement. Realization of this is already the beginning of a qualitative leap in be-ing. For the philosophers of senescence 'the final cause' is in technical reason; it is the Father's plan, an endless flow of Xerox copies of the past. But the final cause that *is movement* is in our imaginative-cerebral-emotional-active-creative be-ing.

An unwitting description of the cause of the peace movement's built-in obsolescence was made by biblically based Dan Berrigan during an interview reported in December 1972 [in the *National Catholic Reporter*]:

> This seminary [Union Theological in New York] is like a playpen. I see signs in the elevators and in the halls, signs about raking leaves, sherry parties, *women's liberation* [emphasis mine] and so forth, but never anything about the war. It's forgotten. There is, practically speaking, no church resistance to the war anymore. But I can't forget about the war.

Berrigan's commitment and courage are unquestionable. But ...

'raking leaves, sherry parties, women's liberation. . . .' When will they understand? It is rapism that has spawned racism. It is gynocide that gives rise to genocide.

In November 1972, the American people elected Richard Nixon to a landslide victory. December 1972 witnessed the heaviest bombing raids on Hanoi since the beginning of the Vietnam war. When will they understand? Can it be that we are beginning to witness 'the fullness of the Gospel'? The Elected One points us toward the Omega Point. It is a time of warfare between principalities and powers.

On December 20, 1972, the news was telecast that Phil Berrigan was released from prison. Mass was celebrated among a gathering of family and friends. During the Mass, Pete Seeger's song 'Turn, Turn' was sung. The words that came over national television were: 'To everything, turn, turn. . . . A time to kill, a time to heal. . . .' The song, of course, has its origin in the Bible, in Ecclesiastes 3, 1–8. The chapter begins: 'There is a season for everything, a time for every occupation under heaven.' Among the approved dichotomies listed in this wisdom literature:

> A time for killing,
> A time for healing;
> A time for knocking down,
> A time for building. . . .
> A time for loving,
> A time for hating,
> A time for war,
> A time for peace.

And so the eternal circle turns. When will they understand? George Wald has written:

> One has to begin to ask, are there such highly superior techno-logical civilizations elsewhere in the universe, or is there not only a time when such a creature arrives, but a somewhat later time, perhaps not very much later, in which he [sic] departs? That problem now very much concerns us.

One answer is: If they are humanoid creatures, split against themselves by an alienative opposition of opposites in the very depth of their psyches, and if they do not resolve *that* problem, then surely they do depart.

Our planet is inhabited by half-crazed creatures, but there is a consistency in the madness. Virginia Woolf, who died of being both brilliant and female, wrote that women are condemned by society to function as mirrors, reflecting men at twice their actual size. When this basic principle is understood, we can understand something about the dynamics of the Looking Glass society. Let us examine once again the creatures' speech.

That language for millennia has affirmed the fact that Eve was born from Adam, the first among history's unmarried pregnant males who courageously chose childbirth under sedation rather than abortion, consequently obtaining a child-bride. Careful study of the documents recording such achievements of Adam and his sons prepared the way for the arrival of the highest of the higher religions, whose priests took Adam as teacher and model. They devised a sacramental system which functioned magnificently within the sacred House of Mirrors. Graciously, they lifted from women the onerous power of childbirth, christening it 'baptism.' Thus they brought the lowly material function of birth, incompetently and even grudgingly performed by females, to a higher and more spiritual level. Recognizing the ineptitude of females in performing even the humble 'feminine' tasks assigned to them by the Divine Plan, the Looking Glass priests raised these functions to the supernatural level in which they alone had competence. Feeding was elevated to become Holy Communion. Washing achieved dignity in Baptism and Penance. Strengthening became known as Confirmation, and the function of consolation, which the unstable nature of females caused them to perform so inadequately, was raised to a spiritual level and called Extreme Unction. In order to stress the obvious fact that all females are innately disqualified from joining the Sacred Men's Club, the Looking Glass priests made it a rule that their members should wear skirts. To make the point clearer, they reserved special occasions when additional Men's Club attire should be worn. These necessary accoutrements included delicate white lace tops and millinery of prescribed shapes and colors. The leaders were required to wear silk hose, pointed hats, crimson dresses and ermine capes, thereby stressing detachment from lowly material things and dedication to the exercise of spiritual talent. They thus became revered models of spiritual transsexualism.

These anointed Male Mothers, who naturally are called Fathers, felt maternal concern for the women entrusted to their pastoral care. Although females obviously are by nature incompetent and prone to mental and emotional confusion, they are required by the Divine Plan as vessels to contain the seeds of men so that men can be born and then supernaturally (correctly) reborn as citizens of the

Heavenly Kingdom. Therefore in charity the priests encouraged women to throw themselves gratefully into their unique role as containers for the sons of the sons of the Son of God. Sincerely moved by the fervor of their own words, the priests educated women to accept this privilege with awe-struck humility.

Since the Protestant Reformation, spiritual Looking Glass education has been modernized in some rooms of the House of Mirrors. Reformed Male Mothers gradually came to feel that Maleness was overstressed by wearing dresses all the time and even decided to include a suitable proportion of females (up to one half of one percent) among their membership, thereby stressing that the time for Male Snobbism was over and the time for Democracy had come. They also came to realize that they could be just as supernatural without being hemmed in by a stiff sacramental system. They could give birth spiritually, heal and console, and give maternal advice. They therefore continued the Looking Glass tradition of Mother Adam while at the same time making a smooth transition to The Modern Age.

Thus, Western culture was gracefully prepared by its Supernatural Mothers called Fathers to see all things supernaturally, that is, to perceive the world backward clearly. In fact, so excellent had been our education that this kind of thinking has become like second nature for almost everybody. No longer in need of spiritual guidance, our culture has come of age. This fact is evident to anyone who will listen to it when it talks. Its statesmen clear-headedly affirm the fact that this is 'the Free World.' Its newscasters accurately report that there has been fighting in the demilitarized zone, that several people were killed in a nonviolent demonstration, that 'our nation' is fighting to bring peace to Southeast Asia. Its psychiatrists proclaim that the entire society is in fact a mental institution and applaud this fact as a promising omen of increasing health for their profession.

In the Looking Glass society females, that is, Magnifying Mirrors, play a crucial role. But males have realized that it would serve no good purpose if this were to become known by females, who then might stop looking into the toy mirrors they have been taught to use incessantly. They might then begin looking inside or outside or backward or forward. Instead of settling for the vanity of parakeets they might fall into the sin of pride and refuse to be Magnifying Mirrors any longer.

The females, in the terrifying, exhilarating experience of becoming rather than reflecting, would discover that they too have been infected by the dynamics of the Mirror World. Having learned only to mirror, they would find in themselves reflections of the sickness in their masters. They would find themselves doing the same things, fighting the same way. Looking inside for something there, they would be confused by what at first would appear to be an endless Hall of Mirrors. What to copy? What model to imitate? Where to look? What is a mere mirror to do? But wait – How could a mere mirror even frame such a question? The question itself is the beginning of an answer that keeps unfolding itself. The question-answer is a verb, and when one begins to move in the current of the verb, of the Verb, she knows that she is not a mirror. Once she knows this she knows it so deeply that she cannot completely forget. She knows it so deeply that she has to say it to her sisters. What if more and more of her sisters should begin to hear and to see and to speak?

This would be a disaster. It would throw the whole society backward into the future. Without Magnifying Mirrors all around, men would have to look inside and outside. They would start to look inside, wondering what was wrong with them. They would have to look outside because without the mirrors they would begin to receive impressions from real Things out there. They would even have to look at women, instead of reflections. This would be confusing and they would be forced to look inside again, only to have the harrowing experience of finding *there* the Eternal Woman, the Perfect Parakeet. Desperately looking outside again, they would find that the Parakeet is no longer *out there*. Dashing back inside, males would find other horrors: All of the other Others – the whole crowd – would be in there: the lazy niggers, the dirty Chicanos, the greedy Jews, faggots and dykes, plus the entire crowd of Communists and the backward population of the Third World. Looking outward again, mirrorless males would be forced to see – people. Where to go? Paroxysm toward the Omega Point? But without the Magnifying Mirror even that last refuge is gone. What to do for relief? Send more bombing missions? But no. It is pointless to be killing The Enemy after you find out The Enemy is yourself.

But the Looking Glass Society is still there, bent on killing itself off. It is still ruled by God the Father who, gazing at his magnified reflections, believes in his superior size. I say 'believes,' because the reflection now occasionally seems to be diminished and so he has to make a renewed act of faith in Himself.

We have been locked in this Eden of his far too long. If we stay much longer, life *will* depart from this planet. The freedom to fall out of Eden will cost a mirror-shattering experience. The freedom-becoming-survival of our species will require a continual, communal striving in be-ing. This means forging the great chain of be-ing in sisterhood that can surround nonbeing, forcing it to shrink back into itself. The cost of failure is Nothing.

Is this the war to end wars? The power of sisterhood is not war-power. There have been and will be conflicts, but the Final Cause causes not by conflict but by attraction. Not by the attraction of a Magnet that is All There, but by the creative drawing power of the Good Who is self-communicating Be-ing. Who is the Verb from whom, in whom, and with whom all true movements move.

Rosemary R. Ruether · *Mistress of Heaven*

Rosemary Ruether, *New Woman/New Earth*, Dove Communications, Australia and Seabury Press, NY 1975. Copyright © 1975 by the Seabury Press, Inc. Used by permission of the publisher

In 1974 Pope Paul VI proposed that Christianity already had a model of the liberated woman in the Virgin Mary. Although few feminists are likely to respond to the figure of Mary because the Pope told them to, nevertheless women, Protestants as much as Catholics, are taking a second look at Mariology to see what positive content for women might exist in this solitary feminine symbol in what appears otherwise a solidly patriarchal religion. Some years ago the Protestant theologian Paul Tillich suggested that Protestantism was too one-sidedly masculine and needed some of the balancing elements of the feminine symbols that existed in Catholicism. The psychologist C. G. Jung hailed the doctrine of the assumption of Mary as the symbolic reintegration of the fatal polarities in Western consciousness between masculine and feminine, body and spirit, earth and heaven.

In her book *Beyond God the Father*, Mary Daly rejects Christology as a redemptive symbol for women, but suggests that redemptive content can be found in a new look at mariological doctrines. Mary's virginity can be understood as the symbol of female autonomy, her completeness and integrity in herself, apart from the male. The doctrine of the immaculate conception counteracts the myth of woman as Eve, the cursed source of sin. Immaculately conceived woman is woman without sin, good in her true, created nature. She is woman as norm of perfected and authentic humanity. The assumption overcomes the hierarchical split between soul and body, male and female. It reintegrates humanity as androgynous person-hood and redeemed body.

Yet despite these liberating possibilities of Mariology, feminists also realize that it is churches with a high Mariology which are most negative to women. It is the Protestant churches without Mariology which ordain women. Mariology operates socially as a right-wing rallying cry among Catholics. It is used as a way of condemning the liberal personal and political mores of the 'modern world.' Mariology, as it is used by the clergy, seems antithetical to the liberation of women. Whose side is Mary on?

Mary, the mother of Jesus, was to become the personal figure around whome all these types of feminine images in the theological tradition were to be gathered together. In Latin theology the ecclesiological and mystical modes predominate, while, at least officially, the idea of a feminine aspect of God was not allowed. Despite its exalta-tion of language, Mary remains a symbol of the self and the community in relation to God, or a maternal mediator between the patriarchal Lord of Heaven and the faithful of the Church. She is not a feminine divine hypostasis. The key mariological doctrines are Mary as the new Eve, her perpetual virginity, her divine maternity, her bodily assumption into heaven, Mary as the mediatrix of all graces, and her immaculate conception.

The New Testament spends little time on Mary as a figure in herself. Even her virginity, in the nativity narratives of Luke and Matthew, is in the context of christological, not mariological, interests. The focus is the virgin birth of Jesus. The virgin birth, theologically, means that the advent of Christ is solely the work of God and is not produced by the works of man (males). Christ, divine grace, comes from above, and is not the product of human history. Since the focus was christological, it could coexist for several centuries with the tradition that Mary, after Jesus' birth, had natural children. The brothers and sisters of Jesus, mentioned in various places in the Gospels, Acts, and Paul, were recognized in the early Church as natural siblings of Jesus. One of these, James, the Lord's brother, became the leader of the Jerusalem community. Matthew's Gospel clearly assumes a normal married sexual life of Mary and Joseph after Jesus' birth (Matt. 1.25).

Aside from the nativity stories, Mary appears in the synoptics only in the pejorative scene where she and the brothers come to speak to Jesus, apparently trying to persuade him to leave his preaching and return home. The family of Jesus are presented in the Gospels as non-believers and Jesus responds by repudiating his natural family for his spiritual brothers and sisters. The Marys of the synoptic crucifixion stores are Mary Magdalene and apparently Mary the mother of James the Younger, rather than Jesus' mother, as are the Marys of the resurrection stories. Only John includes Mary, Jesus' mother, at the crucifixion, in a story that established John as Jesus' heir. Mary also appears in John's story of the marriage feast of Cana, again to be somewhat rebuked for making a presumptuous request. Acts includes Mary and the brothers at Pentecost showing that they were known to be believers in the early Jerusalem community. At what point they enter the believing community from their status of unbelievers during Jesus' ministry is not made known. Nevertheless it is clear that the early historical tradition did not exalt Mary. The feminine figure closest to Jesus was Mary Magdalene. The exaltation of the image of a close relationship between Jesus and his mother in the later tradition has had the effect of suppressing in Christian memory this relationship of Jesus with his female friends and disciples, especially Mary Magdalene, who in all four Gospels is the central female figure of the resurrection stories. Mother Mary is not mentioned in Paul or the other New Testament writings. The dramatic image of the woman in Revelation 12 stands for the Church, although its imagery, drawn from the Isis tradition of the Queen of Heaven, would later be applied to Mary.

At this point we must re-evaluate the meaning of Mariology as a liberating symbol for women. Mariology has its appeal for males because it enshrines the dominant ego and active principle as masculine in relation to women, who become the symbol of passive dependency upon the male. Mariology also allows the male to experience this type of 'femininity' himself. The most patriarchal theologian can experience himself as passive, receptive, the receptacle of divine grace in relation to God. Receptivity is not a bad thing. Indeed it is a capacity which the mature self must develop. But the patriarchal split between activity and passivity along hierarchical sexist lines destroys authentic receptivity. Receptivity is equated with powerlessness, dependency, and self-hatred, whereas authentic receptivity is only possible from a position of autonomy and self-esteem.

The sexist model of activity and receptivity is sado-masochistic, inculcating domination of subordinates, dependency upon superiors. Males also experience this type of 'femininity' in relation to superiors, but one must question whether this constitutes a healthy wholeness. Moreover, the sexist split in the male psyche demands the generic repression of wholeness in women as a group. By equating powerless passivity with 'femininity,' women are made to be specialists in self-abnegating, auxiliary modes of existence, while males monopolize the effective feedback from *both* forms of experience. Feminists, therefore, must be suspicious of males, especially religious leaders, who too quickly say, 'We too need to experience our "feminine side."' As long as the 'feminine' is equated with the 'nature' of women, but the passive, auxiliary 'side' of men, this formulation of 'androgyny' can only reinforce the traditional model of women as nurturers of a selfhood that can appear only in men.

The liberation of women, as well as men, from sexist hierarchicalism cannot happen as long as this symbolism of masculinity and feminity remains. This symbolism must ever rob women of human integrity, while men, even in their passivity, are given a sadomasochistic model of human relations. The entire psychodynamics of relationships must be entirely transformed, so that activity is not identified with domination, split from a receptivity as dependency. We must envision a new model of reciprocity in which we actualize ourselves by the same processes that we support the autonomy and actualization of others. This demands not only a transvaluation in psychic imagery, but a revolution in power relations between the sexes, representing all power relations of domination and subordination. The symbol for this is not an 'androgyny' that still preserves sexist dualism, but that whole personhood in which women can be both I and Thou.

Mariology cannot be a liberating symbol for women as long as it preserves this meaning of 'femininity' that is the complementary underside of masculine domination. Mariology becomes a liberating symbol for women only when it is seen as a radical symbol of a new humanity freed from hierarchical power relations, including that of God and humanity. It is here that the revolutionary side of the image of Mary appears, as the representative of the original and eschatological humanity that is repressed from existence within patriarchy, the culture of domination and subjugation. Woman becomes the symbol of the unknown possibility of a humanity beyond and outside the entire system of such a world. Sophia is the matrix and the Ground of Being of the Father God before patriarchy. She is the perfection of humanity beyond the horizon of grace mediated by masculine power symbols of domination. Mary stands for the eschatological humanity of the new covenant: that 'new thing' which God has created on earth, 'the female overcomes the warrior' (Jer. 31.22). In such a vision the power symbols of God and Christ are meaningful only when they represent the abnegation of domination and the identification with the oppressed.

Mary, in turn, as the *persona* of the new Israel, does not represent the feminine, but that original wholeness of humanity destroyed by sin, for sexism is the original sin of domination that destroys the image of God in humanity and the world. Woman, as the representative of the first and last suppressed person in history, stands for the Church, the new humanity whose nature and possibility remains unrevealed or distorted in a Christianity still modeled on sexist dualisms. She is the reconciled wholeness of women and men, nature and humans, creation and God in the new heaven and the new earth. In her, God already shows mercy and might: the proud are scattered in the imagination of their hearts; the mighty are put down from their thrones, while the humiliated are lifted up; the rich are sent away empty, and the hungry are filled with good things. With such a Mary women might even be able to say: 'My soul magnifies the Lord and my spirit rejoices in God my Savior' (Luke 1.46–47). But the Mary whom we should venerate may not be Mother Mary, the woman who represents the patriarchal view that woman's only claim to fame is the capacity to have babies, the relationship which Jesus himself rejected. The Mary who represents the Church, the liberated humanity, may, rather, be the repressed and defamed Mary of the Christian tradition, Mary Magdalene, friend and disciple of Jesus, the first witness of the resurrection, the revealer of the Christian Good News. Blessed is the womb that bore thee, the paps that gave thee suck? Nay, rather, blessed is she who heard the Word of God and kept it (cf. Luke 11.27–28).

Sheila Collins · *A Feminist Reading of History*

Sheila Collins, 'A Feminist Reading of History', *Radical Religion*, Vol. 1, No. 2, 1974, pp.12–13, 17. Used by permission of the author

Paul Freire has pointed out that all education is political. I would go further to state that all theology is ultimately political. The way human communities reify the transcendent and determine the categories of good and evil have more to do with the power dynamics of the social systems which create the theologies than with spontaneous revelation of truth from another quarter. As Peter Berger has shown, all symbol systems are creations of the world, religion offering the most potent legitimation of these humanly constructed worlds. This is not to deny that there may be another reality lurking on the edges of consciousness which now and then breaks through. However, when 'revelation' becomes solidified, in doctrine, creed and ritual, it too often becomes the tool of the legislators of morality, who thereby maintain themselves in power against challenges to the worldview that sustains them.

We are all familiar with white establishment Christian piety, which uses the image of Christ as 'gentle Jesus meek and mild' or as 'the Prince of Peace' to condemn oppressed peoples' violent attempts to throw off the yoke of oppression. These establishment Christians wreak their own more subtle forms of violence, applauding it as 'law and order.' Politically liberal or radical men, however, often find it harder to comprehend another aspect of oppression within Judeo-Christianity. Despite its ostensibly noble impulses to justice, liberation and universal love, the Judeo-Christian religious system has been used to crush other historical impulses which might have added a much needed balance to the psychic development of Western culture.

Having seen through the power games played by Judeo-Christian theologians and philosophers, women today are searching for a new basis for values, a new mythology and anthropology, a new way of imaging transcendence. We want to be sure that the value system we look to allows for our own self-actualization, but we also are concerned that it is not used to subjugate others. We are concerned for personal tranformation, but we also want to change the systemic causes of oppression. We are concerned for justice and freedom in the human community, but we are also concerned with respect for the earth, without which we are all doomed to extinction. In short, we seek for diversity within a unified world, for a sense of wholeness of creation.

Where do we turn to discover the roots of that wholeness? Where do we begin to establish a new mythology and symbolization? For in spite of our desire not to be bound by the old mythologies and images, we seem unable to escape the creations of meaning worlds. We humans are all theologizers and philosophizers whether we like it or not. Perhaps now, however, we can start out on a more self-conscious and, therefore hopefully, more just basis. We openly acknowledge the self-interest involved in our critiques of present systems. We know that our theologizing and philosophizing will have political implications, and in admitting our biases from the outset, perhaps we are one step ahead in the search for a just order.

I would like to suggest that a feminist rereading of history, in consonance with our own unfettered experience of life, may be one of the sources of new insight and inspiration. Simone Weil, a brilliant thinker who has largely been ignored (because she was a woman?) once pointed out that history is 'nothing but a compilation of the depositions made by assassins with respect to their victims and themselves.' If we accept Ms. Weil's analysis as valid, then the feminist movement provides us with the most radical departure for a critique of all our institutions and value systems. Women have always been extra-environmentals; that is, we have never had our own story told, at least within recorded history. We have always been the victims, for whom depositions have been made by our male conquerors.

A rereading of history through feminist eyes has much to teach us about the possibility for human hope, liberation and justice. A feminist rereading commits women and men to more honesty and self-consciousness about the sources of our values and the operation of our ethical system. By opening up to consciousness those impulses in the life of humanity which have been ignored, distorted or repudiated we see if a fresh appropriation might not offer needed insight in our present circumstances. The feminist view will make us more humble about the uses to which history and tradition have been put, especially by our Western religious institutions, for whom history as the Divine Event has been the *sine qua non* of all saving knowledge. A feminist rereading of history should also caution us against making the mistakes that male-led movements for social change, whether of the right or left, have made for the past three millennia.

I would like to concentrate here on one small part of the re-evaluation of history which needs to be made by feminists, the period which spans the development and eventual triumph of monotheism in ancient Israel. This is a significant period to re-evalute, because it is the source of one of the most powerful symbolizations of human liberation and fulfilment which has been and is now being used by those who are struggling for freedom and justice in the world, namely, the symbol of the Exodus.

Now admittedly, the Exodus is an appealing symbol: a people freed from an oppressive bondage and passing over into a promised land. One can readily see how appropriate that image was for black slaves in the 19th century, who explored all of its ramifications in preaching, prayer and song. The symbol, for want of a better one, has even been used by feminist theologians (see Mary Daly's *Beyond God the Father*), albeit in a more obtuse way. I would submit, however, that such an image is inappropriate for feminists and possibly for blacks as well. We cannot blame the slaves for using the only paradigm of freedom available to them at the time. Could they have known their own history, however, they might better have chosen as a paradigm of hope and fulfillment the story of those slaves who escaped from the ships and founded an entirely new black culture in British Guiana, retaining most of their African roots and traditions in the process. Such a paradigm might have saved American blacks the long and ignominious hassle of attempting to imitate the white man's ways, an attempt which has only in the last decade been repudiated.

As feminists, we must be careful that the symbols and paradigms we use to inspire and sustain us are not those which participate in our own subjugation, or in that of others if we are concerned for justice. The Exodus may be just such a symbol. Most of us who reflect on that symbol recall its freedom-generating impulse, but we forget the other half of the equation, which only a feminist reading of history will allow us to see. The 'Promised Land' into which the Israelites were led by their God was not an empty wasteland waiting for the Chosen People to occupy and domesticate, but a land already occupied by peoples who had their own religious and political systems which the Israelites, as the Old Testament faithfully records, fought against and eventually triumphed over. The bellicose deeds of Joshua, Barak, Judah, Gideon, and countless others are all favorably recorded by the Old Testament. We read that it was, indeed, God's will that the Israelites slay tens of thousands, that they burn cities, rape women, and cut off the enemy's ears. We read also that whenever the armies of the Israelites were defeated, it was taken as a sign of God's punishment for their (unexplained) evil ways.

But I am increasingly concerned with the evidence I see all around me of the continuation of mechanistic thinking and perception, in Marxists as well as in movements on the Right. Women must become the vanguard of a different kind of revolution, and in it the wholeness of nature, the rhythm and balance so necessary to sustain life, must guide us. It will be a revolution which uses the body and the mind, the emotions and the intellect, imagination and logic, kindness as well as anger. We will find the sacred in the profane and learn to transform both the personal and the political, our relationship to the earth as well as to each other. We need to learn to discriminate, yes, to cast blame where it is due, and to exorcize when that is needed; but we do not need to throw out the baby with the bath! If anything, our training as females should remind us that the dirty water may have to be thrown out, but we always need another supply; for the baby gets dirty quite often and needs to be washed again and again. Rhythm. Balance. Process. No more games of Chosen People, of Either/Or for us. The world is far too small now for that. We will have to teach our world to live with Both/And, or I fear for our survival.

5 · Politics of Mission

Few things are more likely to induce a sense of panic than the news that some public figure has a mission in life. Who would not settle for a little more pragmatism and a little less Moses? Who has not sympathized with D. H. Lawrence: 'Send us no more messiahs'. The ominous implications are that the man with a mission in life actually has designs on our own lives rather than his own. He knows better than we do what problems we face and how they must be solved. He knows how incomplete our lives are and how they are to be fulfilled. He knows, despite our protestations that we are all right as we are or that his cure is worse than the disease. Or rather he sees in our very protestations just how much we do need his help.

As often happens, this is not a peculiarly religious phenomenon, but religion can intensify it and elevate it to new levels. Of course there is no objection to offering help or even trying to convince people that they should choose some alternative in life. In his speeches *On Religion* Schleiermacher distinguished between a 'praiseworthy zeal for conversion' and 'that wild irreligious mania for conversion which easily degenerates into persecution'. The one originates in a genuine concern for other people, but the other is concerned with a body-count and originates in the psychological needs of the missionary. The one is content if the individual becomes himself, the other is not content until the individual is replaced by a replica of the missionary.

A decade ago it was fashionable to criticize Western missionary activity in black Africa. The missionaries, it was confidently reported, had simply taken passage on the gun-boats and legitimized the imposition of colonialism on the gullible natives. Gullibility is more characteristic of anyone who believed that ideological tale. Religion was an important element during the colonization and the decolonization of Africa, but it was not simply a weapon of the new rulers. It often provided a means by which Africans dealt with the crisis of culture, the disturbing expansion of new horizons. Matthew Schoffeleers has well illustrated this in his treatment of the M'Bona cult at Khulubvi, Malawi (in *The Historical Study of African Religion* ed. T. O. Ranger and I. N. Kimambo, Heinemann 1972). The cosmic significance of M'Bona was considerably expanded through the influence of biblical themes, including the belief that God had two sons, Jesus for the white parts of the world and M'Bona for the black. (This is similar to the influence of Babylonian religion on the Jews of the Exile.) In other instances there was little theological adjustment, but being converted to Christianity provided a social and economic benefit. According to Bethwell Ogot this would be true in the case of the Padhola of Uganda. Their God was originally called Jok (which throws no light on President Amin's admiration for all things Scottish). Nor was this unique to Christianity. The same could be noted of Islam in, for example, northern Mozambique. By the nineteenth century religion was a discrete phenomenon in an increasingly secular Western culture. It could be advanced by missionaries as a thing in itself. However, it was received in Africa, where religion was still the fabric of the culture. Robert Horton therefore sees both Christianity and Islam in this context as catalysts, 'i.e. stimulators and accelerators of changes which were "in the air" anyway' ('African Conversion', *Africa*, XLI, 2, 1971).

Such effects were not consciously intended by Christian missionaries, but they did make it possible for many Africans to preserve their identity and successfully make the transition to the new world to which colonization introduced them. During the last twenty years there has been a revival of traditional African religion by nationalists who wish to undermine the influence of Christianity and its strong links with colonial powers. Anthony Wilkinson indicates how traditional religion has become an issue in the war in Rhodesia. The white regime issued a pamphlet to tribesmen sympathetic to the guerrillas: 'Mhondoro, your tribal spirit, has sent a message to say that your ancestral spirits are very dissatisfied with you' (*Southern Africa: The New Politics of Revolution*, Penguin Books 1976). In a country where all mail is censored it seems reasonable that such a message should reach the tribesmen through the Ministry of Information.

An account of the impact of missionaries on Africa would have to include reference to the educational, medical and welfare work which became the foundation of such provisions in modern independent states. But we should also mention the prophetic element which was for example largely instrumental in the resistance of the people of Nyasaland to the imposition and continuation of the Central Africa Federation.

The picture of Christianity taking over the natives and delivering them as passive houseboys to the colonists has no basis in fact. Its relationship to social and political developments in the continent has been much more varied than this. Yet there has been an effect which is more subtle to identify and which may have a more lasting effect. It concerns the form in which Christianity has been introduced.

One of my African students came to me one day looking very worried. She told me that she was greatly troubled over the problem of free will. She should not have been, yet such was the presentation of Christianity that to be truly a Christian meant not only acting like Europeans and believing what Europeans believed, but being concerned over the things that concerned Europeans. Now throughout the centuries Christianity has changed many times. It has touched upon the deep concerns of particular ages. To a culture fervently expecting the Kingdom it has proclaimed the Messiah; to a culture distraught over death and the meaning of life it has proclaimed eternal life in the Logos. To a culture fixated on crusades it has proclaimed the Warrior Prince. To a culture racked with guilt it has proclaimed justification by faith alone. The problem of free will was strongly felt by a culture discovering the iron laws of nature. Christian faith will not be good news unless it answers the problems of the culture.

Previously we were considering missionary work in Africa, but of course Europe has largely turned away from Christianity. There is little missionary work in Britain. The reason for this is that the people are impervious to the form of Christianity presented to them. Does this indicate their sinful state? Perhaps, but it may well be that the gospel proclaimed to them attempts to deal with issues which belonged to the nineteenth rather than twentieth centuries. Never has there been a century with so many 'issues', yet the gospel is not addressed to them. The effect of the mission of the church is therefore conservative, either continuing to present the agenda of yesteryear, or trying to persuade responsible people that religion is above the ambiguities of this life.

Unfortunately this form of Christianity has been exported to Africa. On the previous model, we should expect Christianity to be addressing the lively issues which involve Africans today. Ominously, something else is happening. As one colporteur asked, 'Why do the people give up religion when they go to the city?' Why not? It is a European form of Christianity – and in European cities few people go to church. Unless new forms of Christianity are allowed to emerge, encouraged to emerge, then throughout the world those who live in the secular city will be denied religion. The social and political consequences of mission, home and abroad, are likely to be bad news.

Ivan Illich · *The Seamy Side of Charity*

Selections from Chapter 5 of Ivan Illich, *Celebration of Awareness*, Doubleday, NY and Calder & Boyars 1971. Copyright © 1969 by Ivan D. Illich. Reprinted by permission of Doubleday & Company Inc. and Marion Boyars

Church policy makers in the United States must face up to the socio-political consequences involved in their well-intended missionary ventures. They must review their vocation as Christian theologians and their actions as Western politicians.

Men and money sent with missionary motivation carry a foreign Christian image, a foreign pastoral approach and a foreign political message. They also bear the mark of North American capitalism of the 1950s. Why not, for once, consider the seamy side of charity; weigh the inevitable burdens foreign help imposes on the South American Church; taste the bitterness of the damage done by our sacrifices? . . .

This kind of foreign generosity has enticed the Latin American Church into becoming a satellite to North Atlantic cultural phenomena and policy. Increased apostolic resources intensified the need for this continued flow and created islands of apostolic well-being, each day further beyond the capacity of local support. The Latin American Church flowers anew by returning to what the Conquest stamped her: a colonial plant that blooms because of foreign cultivation. Instead of learning how to get along with less money or else close up shop, bishops are being trapped into needing more money now and bequeathing an institution impossible to run in the future. Education, the one type of investment that could give long-range returns, is conceived mostly as training for bureaucrats who will maintain the existing apparatus.

Recently I saw an example of this in a large group of Latin American priests who had been sent to Europe for advanced degrees. In order to relate the Church to the world, nine-tenths of these men were studying teaching methods – catechetics, pastoral theology or canon law – and thereby not directly advancing their knowledge of either the Church or the world. Only a few studied the Church in its history and sources, or the world as it is.

It is easy to come by big sums to build a new church in a jungle or a high school in a suburb, and then to staff the plants with new missionaries. A patently irrelevant pastoral system is artificially and expensively sustained, while basic research for a new and vital one is considered an extravagant luxury. Scholarships for non-ecclesiastical humanist studies, seed money for imaginative pastoral experimentation, grants for documentation and research to make specific constructive criticism all run the frightening risk of threatening our temporal structures, clerical plants and 'good business' methods.

Even more surprising than churchly generosity for churchly concern is a second source of money. A decade ago the Church was like an impoverished *grande dame* trying to keep up an imperial tradition of almsgiving from her reduced income. In the more than a century since Spain lost Latin America, the Church has steadily lost government grants, patrons' gifts and, finally, the revenue from its former lands. According to the colonial concept of charity, the Church lost its power to help the poor. It came to be considered a historical relic, inevitably the ally of conservative politicians.

By 1966 almost the contrary seems true – at least, at first sight. The Church has become an agent trusted to run programmes aimed at social change. It is committed enough to produce some results. But when it is threatened by real change, it withdraws rather than permit social awareness to spread like wildfire. The smothering of the Brazilian radio schools by a high Church authority is a good example.

Thus Church discipline assures the donor that his money does twice the job in the hands of a priest. It will not evaporate, nor will it be accepted for what it is: publicity for private enterprise and indoctrination to a way of life that the rich have chosen as suitable for the poor. The receiver inevitably gets the message: the 'padre' stands on the side of W. R. Grace and Company, Esso, the Alliance for Progress, democratic government, the AFL–CIO and whatever is holy in the Western pantheon.

Opinion is divided, of course, on whether the Church went heavily into social projects because it could thus obtain funds 'for the poor', or whether it went after the funds because it could thus contain Castroism and assure its institutional respectability. By becoming an 'official' agency of one kind of progress, the Church ceases to speak for the underdog who is outside all agencies but who is an ever growing majority. By accepting the power to help, the Church necessarily must denounce a Camilo Torres, who symbolizes the power of renunciation. Money thus builds the Church a 'pastoral' structure beyond its means and makes it a political power ...

Massive, indiscriminate importation of clergy helps the ecclesiastical bureaucracy survive in its own colony, which every day becomes more foreign and comfortable. This immigration helps to transform the old-style hacienda of God (on which the people were only squatters) into the Lord's supermarket, with catechisms, liturgy and other means of grace heavily in stock. It makes contented consumers out of vegetating peasants, demanding clients out of former devotees. It lines the sacred pockets, providing refuge for men who are frightened by secular responsibility.

Churchgoers, accustomed to priests, novenas, books and culture from Spain (quite possibly to Franco's picture in the rectory), now meet a new type of executive, administrative and financial talent promoting a certain type of democracy as the Christian ideal. The people soon see that the Church is distant, alienated from them – an imported, specialized operation, financed from abroad, which speaks with a holy, because foreign, accent.

This foreign transfusion – and the hope for more – gave ecclesiastical pusillanimity a new lease of life, another chance to make the archaic and colonial system work. If North America and Europe send enough priests to fill the vacant parishes, there is no need to consider laymen – unpaid for part-time work – to fulfil most evangelical tasks; no need to re-examine the structure of the parish, the function of the priest, the Sunday obligation and clerical sermon; no need to explore the use of the married diaconate, new forms of celebration of the Word and Eucharist, and intimate familial celebrations of conversion to the gospel in the milieu of the home. The promise of more clergy is like a bewitching siren. It makes the chronic surplus of clergy in Latin America invisible and it makes it impossible to diagnose this surplus as the gravest illness of the Church. Today, this pessimistic evaluation is slightly altered by a courageous and imaginative few – non-Latins among them – who see, study and strive for true reform.

A large proportion of Latin American Church personnel are presently employed in private institutions that serve the middle and upper classes and frequently produce highly respectable profits; this on a continent where there is a desperate need for teachers, nurses and social workers in public institutions that serve the poor. A large part of the clergy are engaged in bureaucratic functions, usually related to peddling sacraments, sacramentals and superstitious 'blessings'. Most of them live in squalor. The Church, unable to use its personnel in pastorally meaningful tasks, cannot even support its priests and the 670 bishops who govern them. Theology is used to justify this system, canon law to administer it and foreign clergy to create a world-wide consensus on the necessity of its continuation.

A healthy sense of values empties the seminaries and the ranks of the clergy much more effectively than does a lack of discipline and generosity. In fact, the new mood of well-being makes the ecclesiastical career more attractive to the self-seeker. Bishops turn servile beggars, become tempted to organize safaris, and hunt out foreign priests and funds for constructing such anomalies as minor seminaries. As long as such expeditions succeed, it will be difficult, if not impossible, to take the emotionally harder road: to ask ourselves honestly if we need such a game.

Exporting Church employees to Latin America masks a universal and unconscious fear of a new Church. North and South American authorities, differently motivated but equally fearful, become accomplices in maintaining a clerical and irrelevant Church. Sacralizing employees and property, this Church becomes progressively more blind to the possibilities of sacralizing person and community.

It is hard to help by refusing to give alms. I remember once having stopped food distribution from sacristies in an area where there was great hunger. I still feel the sting of an accusing voice saying: 'Sleep well for the rest of your life with the death of dozens of children on your conscience.' Even some doctors prefer aspirins to radical surgery. They feel no guilt having the patient die of cancer, but fear the risk of applying the knife. The courage needed today is that expressed by Daniel Berrigan, S.J., writing of Latin America: 'I suggest we stop sending anyone or anything for three years and dig in and face our mistakes and find out how not to canonize them.'

From six years' experience in training hundreds of foreign missionaries assigned to Latin America, I know that real volunteers increasingly want to face the truth that puts their faith to the test. Superiors who shift personnel by their administrative decisions but do not have to live with the ensuing deceptions are emotionally handicapped facing these realities.

The United States Church must face the painful side of generosity: the burden that a life gratuitously offered imposes on the recipient. The men who go to Latin America must humbly accept the possibility that they are useless or even harmful, although they give all they have. They must accept the fact that a limping ecclesiastical assistance programme uses them as palliatives to ease the pain of a cancerous structure, the only hope being that the prescription will give the organism enough time and rest to initiate a spontaneous healing. It is far more probable that the pharmacist's pill will both stop the patient from seeking a surgeon's advice and addict him to the drug.

Foreign missionaries increasingly realize that they heeded a call to plug the holes in a sinking ship because the officers did not dare launch the life rafts. Unless this is clearly seen, men who obediently offer the best years of their lives will find themselves tricked into a useless struggle to keep a doomed liner afloat as it limps through uncharted seas.

We must acknowledge that missionaries can be pawns in a world ideological struggle and that it is blasphemous to use the gospel to prop up any social or political system. When men and money are sent into a society within the framework of a programme, they bring ideas that live after them. It has been pointed out, in the case of the Peace Corps, that the cultural mutation catalysed by a small foreign group might be more effective than all the immediate services it renders. The same can be true of the North American missionary – close to home, having great means at his disposal, frequently on a short-term assignment – who moves into an area of intense United States cultural and economic colonization. He is part of this sphere of influence and, at times, intrigue. Through the United States missionary, the United States shadows and colours the public image of the Church. The influx of United States missionaries coincides with the Alliance for Progress, Camelot and CIA projects and looks like a baptism of all three. The Alliance appears directed by Christian justice and is not seen for what it is: a deception designed to maintain the *status quo*, albeit variously motivated. During the programme's first five years, the net capital leaving Latin America has tripled. The programme is too small to permit even the achievement of a threshold of sustained growth. It is a bone thrown to the dog, that he remain quiet in the back-yard of the Americas.

Within these realities, the United States missionary tends to fulfil the traditional role of a colonial power's lackey chaplain. The dangers implicit in Church use of foreign money assume the proportion of caricature when this aid is administered by a 'gringo' to keep the 'underdeveloped' quiet. It is, of course, too much to ask of most Americans that they make sound, clear and outspoken criticisms of United States socio-political aggression in Latin America, even more difficult that they do so without the bitterness of the expatriate or the opportunism of the turncoat.

Groups of United States missionaries cannot avoid projecting the image of 'United States outposts'. Only individual Americans mixed in with local men could avoid this distortion. The missionary of necessity is an 'undercover' agent – albeit unconscious – for United States social and political consensus. But, consciously and purposely, he wishes to bring the values of his Church to South America; adaptation and selection seldom reach the level of questioning the values themselves.

The situation was not so ambiguous ten years ago, when in good conscience mission societies were channels for the flow of traditional United States Church hardware to Latin America. Everything from the Roman collar to parochial schools, from United States catechisms to Catholic universities, was considered saleable merchandise in the new Latin American market. Not much salesmanship was needed to convince the Latin bishops to give the 'Made in USA' label a try.

In the meantime however, the situation has changed considerably. The United States Church is shaking from the first findings of a scientific and massive self-evaluation. Not only methods and institutions, but also the ideologies that they imply, are subject to examination and attack. The self-confidence of the American ecclesiastical salesman is therefore shaky. We see the strange paradox of a man attempting to implant, in a really different culture, structures and programmes that are now rejected in the country of their origin. (I recently heard of a Catholic grammar school being planned by United States personnel in a Central American city parish where there are already a dozen public schools.)

There is an opposite danger, too. Latin America can no longer tolerate being a haven for United States liberals who cannot make their point at home, an outlet for apostles too 'apostolic' to find their vocation as competent professionals within their own community. The hardware salesman threatens to dump second-rate imitations of parishes, schools and catechisms – outmoded even in the United States – all around the continent. The travelling escapist threatens further to confuse a foreign world with his superficial protests, which are not viable even at home.

The American Church of the Vietnam generation finds it difficult to engage in foreign aid without exporting either its solutions or its problems. Both are prohibitive luxuries for developing nations. Mexicans, to avoid offending the sender, pay high duties for useless or unasked-for gifts sent them by well-meaning American friends. Gift givers must think not of this moment and of this need, but in terms of a full generation of the future effects. Gift planners must ask if the global value of the gift in men, money and ideas is worth the price the recipient will ultimately have to pay for it. As Father Berrigan suggests, the rich and powerful can decide not to give; the poor can hardly refuse to accept. Since almsgiving conditions the beggar's mind, the Latin American bishops are not entirely at fault in asking for misdirected and harmful foreign aid. A large measure of the blame lies with the underdeveloped ecclesiology of United States clerics who direct the 'sale' of American good intentions.

The United States Catholic wants to be involved in an ecclesiologically valid programme, not in subsidiary political and social programmes designed to influence the growth of developing nations according to anybody's social doctrine, be it even described as the Pope's. The heart of the discussion is therefore not *how* to send more men and money, but rather *why* they should be sent at all. The Church, in the meantime, is in no critical danger. We are tempted to shore up and salvage structures rather than question their purpose and truth. Hoping to glory in the works of our hands, we feel guilty, frustrated and angry when part of the building starts to crumble. Instead of believing in the Church, we frantically attempt to construct it according to our own cloudy cultural image. We want to build community, relying on techniques, and are blind to the latent desire for unity that is striving to express itself among men. In fear, we plan *our* Church with statistics, rather than trustingly search for the living Church which is right among us.

Kosuke Koyama · *The Spat-upon Jesus Christ*

Kosuke Koyama, *No Handle on the Cross*, Orbis Books, Maryknoll, and SCM Press 1976, pp.38–39, 91–97

I wish to say that self-denial means 'to live with the *stigma* of Jesus Christ'. This is the theological structure and meaning of self-denial. This is the 'christological' character of self-denial. Do we live with this sign? Is our life continuously made uneasy and insecure (!) because of the *stigma* we bear? 'Out of the depths I cry to thee, O Lord' (Ps. 130.1). My friend the monk walks in Singapore with the *stigma* of the Buddha. He bears the sign of the Buddha. His self-denial is 'buddhalogical'. His orange robes and his empty bag point to the ideal of the monastic life, the value of homelessness that Buddha taught.

He was obviously deeply puzzled by the campaigning behaviour of Christians. In many parts of Asia we come across a 'Crusade for Christ'. In Hong Kong, Singapore, Taiwan, Thailand and Korea crusades come in waves. Asians know intuitively that the holy man Jesus Christ cannot be the man of religious crusade. Strangely Asia knows Jesus Christ as the self-denier. The holy man is the self-denier. Am I just suggesting that the wording 'Crusade for Christ' should be dropped? What I am really aiming at here is to place such campaign psychology of Christians under the light of the New Testament theology of the *stigma* of Jesus Christ. What does the *stigma* of Jesus Christ mean in our evangelism? Every crusade event in Asia accentuates the tragic discrepancy between the 'theology of the *stigma* of Christ' and the 'theology of the crusade for Christ'. In this discrepancy I see an equally serious sign of discrepancy between Asian spirituality and that of the Christian West. In rejecting the 'theology of the crusade for Christ' intuitively and emotionally, the Asians are indicating their genuine openness to the alternative, the theology of the *stigma* of Christ. Asians know what self-denial and *stigma* mean through their own history and experience. The biblical salvation history moves with the sign of the *stigma* of Christ, not with the religious campaign.

You remember Joseph's dream? How his sheaf stood up? Up to now the discussion of the finality of Christ has been predominantly formulated within the framework of Joseph's sweet dream of my-sheaf-stood-up theology. All other religions are supposed to bow down to the upright sheaf of Christianity. Often this thinking has been bolstered by paternalistic-colonial sentiment and language. For example, we hear even in 1975 (!) from the mouths of the proponents of the finality of Jesus Christ that the Asians cannot know the meaning of moral living without the missionaries' Christian instruction! Christians today do not realize how deeply they are still dreaming the pleasing dream of Joseph. That Jesus Christ is the one who is promised to come is a crucified truth. It is not an ordinary truth which can be established by comparative studies. 'But far be it from me to glory except in the cross of our Lord Jesus Christ, by which the world has been crucified to me, and I to the world' (Gal. 6.14). This new self-identity, originating in the 'cross of our Lord Jesus

Christ', points to the one who is promised to come. The crucified truth must be proclaimed by the crucified mind. 'Where two or three are gathered in my name, there am I in the midst of them' (Matt. 18.20). This is the promise given not only to the church but to all the missiological situations in Thailand, Hong Kong and Switzerland, and so on. 'In my name' is the name of the one who suffered. 'There is no other name' means the name of the one who suffered. '. . . kneeling before him they mocked him, . . . they spat upon him, . . . stripped him of the robe . . .' (Matt. 27.28–31). If Jesus Christ was mocked, spat upon and stripped, then his 'finality' is mocked, spat upon and stripped. The 'mocked finality' is, then, the christological finality. But 'the mocked finality' and 'spat-upon finality' do not come under an ordinary concept of finality or primacy.

Jesus is 'the one who is to come', 'there is no other name . . .' and 'where two or three are gathered in my name . . .' point to Jesus Christ who saves the one who mocks him, who cleans the one who spits upon him. The finality of Jesus Christ – what an unusual concept of finality! – grasps us instead of being articulated by us. Church and mission together draw their life from *this name*. The spat-upon Jesus means the spat-upon finality of Jesus. It must mean then the 'spat-upon bishops', 'spat-upon theology', 'spat-upon evangelism', 'spat-upon "combat-against-racism"', 'spat-upon churches'. The finality of Christ and 'being spat-upon' go together! The glory of Christ and 'being spat-upon' go together! Such a concept of finality is in diametrical opposition to the paternalistic mentality. If there is one thing that paternalism cannot take that is this being spat upon.

'To be apostolic' means 'to be ready to be spat upon'. 'We have become, and are now, as the refuse of the world, the off-scouring of all things' (I Cor. 4.13). History can be approached in two ways: the way of spitting upon others and the way of being spat upon by others. History is touched superficially by the former and profoundly by the latter. Ecclesiology and missiology must be rooted in the latter, since the first-born of all things and the first-born of the dead came to us in the latter way. I maintain that to the degree that the church has spat upon other religious faiths and spiritual traditions in Asia, she has become superficial in her christological impact upon the Asian man and history. To the degree that the church has been spat upon, she has become alive in mission and healing in the history.

Jesus before Pilate puzzles us. 'And the chief priests accused him of many things. And Pilate again asked him, "Have you no answer to make? See how many charges they bring against you." But Jesus made no further answer, so that Pilate wondered.' (Mark 15.3–5). Wasn't this an opportunity for Jesus to speak out in his own defence and that of his mission? He remained silent. 'In the beginning was the Word.' This very Word acted as though 'in the beginning was the silence'. At Caesarea Philippi 'he strictly charged the disciples to tell no one that he was the Christ'. This again puzzles us. Why not tell the saving truth to everyone? Is not this an indication Jesus dislikes his 'finality' to be talked about noisily?

Discussions of 'finality', 'superiority' and 'the best religion is Christianity' are motivated by the mind trying to speak about Jesus Christ on the basis of a 'comprehensive' observation. The concepts of finality, superiority and the best presuppose the result of a comprehensive assessment. But theological perception is primarily grace-grasped instead of data-grasped. No handle on the cross! Theological language is symbolical, sacramental and revelatory instead of being comprehensive and comparative. It is so because 'no one has ever seen God; the only Son, who is in the bosom of the Father, he has made him known' (John 1.18). If we should speak of the 'finality' of Jesus Christ, we must know that it is the 'mocked finality', 'hidden finality' and 'crucified finality'. The only Son made God known to us as he gave himself for us.

Let me relate the theology of 'mocked finality' to South East Asian life. The South East Asian traditional style of life, the sense of value, the manner of conducting human relationships, education, transportation, political organization and so on are being disrupted by both positive and negative values which Western civilization has brought in. In this critical-historical moment, South East Asian peoples are engaged in two areas of immense theological importance. Let me express this in New Testament language: they are, first, in the area of 'Come out of the man, you unclean spirit!' (Mark 5.8), and secondly, in the area of 'man shall not live by bread alone, but by every word that proceeds from the mouth of God' (Matt. 4.4; Deut. 8.3).

The poverty-stricken and labour-exploited masses of South East Asia are shouting: 'Come out of the nation, you unclean spirits of corruption, oppression, exploitation and inflation!' The works of the unclean spirit are unmistakably there when corruption paralyses national economy and morality. A twenty-year-old woman, working ten hours a day, draws only five Singapore dollars a day. The rich are getting richer through the sacrifice of the human dignity of the masses. 'Come out of the man, you unclean spirit!' No other passage can be closer to the minds of the frustrated masses. They experience that the unclean spirit is powerful and does not come out easily. But the masses refuse to stop saying 'Come out ...' They 'hope against hope' in the midst of enormous frustration. Here is a reality of 'Christian civilization' which is completely different from the traditional civilization of Christendom. When the masses shout for the exorcism of the unclean spirit, are they not participating in the exorcism of Jesus Christ? Is not this a sign of a great spiritual struggle and awakening? When they say 'Come out of the man, you unclean spirit!' to their exploiters – yes, brutal exploiters – are they not pointing to Jesus Christ, even though they are not aware of his name? Yes. They are not aware of the name of Jesus Christ. But his name is there and his name is the name of the crucified one. This name, the mocked name, spat-upon name is – how remarkable and how strange! – the name that exorcises the evil names. It is mocked by the evil power, yet – or rather because of it! – it is able to stand against the power of evil and make it captive (II Cor. 10.3–5). The mocked name is the very name by which the evil names are cast out!

Modernization is ambiguous in its impact upon the people of South East Asia. It is both 'stone' and 'bread' (Matt. 7.9). The masses have taken notice of the 'bread' character of the impact of modernization. Newly available means of transportation can take a sick child to a hospital fifteen kilometres away, even in the rain. It is 'bread'. Ubiquitous Japanese transistor radios keep the masses informed about economic, political, racial, technological and domestic-international situations. It is 'bread'. Their intake of information has been phenomenally increased. Efficient printing machines placed good quality textbooks in the hands of the millions of South East Asian children. Education has been universalized and upgraded. It is again newly baked 'bread'. Technology has brought running water into kitchens. Telephones eradicated the distances. The people in South East Asia are now beginning to taste the newly-baked modernization 'bread' of all kinds.

The newly baked 'bread' is placed in the context of 'man shall not live by bread alone, but by every word that proceeds from the mouth of god'. Each cultural context of humanity has its own 'word that proceeds from the mouth of God'. Sometimes, it is the voice of human conscience or consensus of the elders of the community. At other times, it is the fundamental creed of Buddhism or Islam, and so on. In each living context, the newly baked 'bread' is examined. How does it stand up to 'every word that proceeds from the mouth of God'? 'Bread alone' is not enough. 'Bread alone' is even dangerous to the welfare of the human spirituality. 'Clothing alone' becomes obscene and perverse. 'Shelter alone' becomes spiritually wasteful 'grand-house-prestige-ism'. 'Sex alone' becomes paralysing sexism. 'Money alone' becomes anti-human exploitative egoism. 'Brain alone' becomes dangerous idolatry of human intelligence. 'Work alone' becomes a system of self-imposed slavery. 'Technology alone' becomes a threat to human life. 'Power alone' becomes destructive power which produces a repressive society. 'Religion alone' becomes a self-righteous human relationship. Bread, clothing, shelter, sex, money, brain, work, technology, power and religion must be illuminated and judged by 'every word that proceeds from the mouth of God'. I am saying that this is happening apart from the explicit biblical word of God. While the people of South East Asia engage in this 'bread alone ...' dispute they do not consciously associate the name of Jesus Christ. Yet it is a deeply biblical theological discussion, since it has to do with the basic welfare of humanity upon this planet. The name of Jesus Christ is there. It is not confessed in faith. But it is there. Where? In all these concrete situations of human life, Jesus Christ is profoundly there since it is impossible to stop the one whose name is spat-upon finality from coming and being there. It is possible to stop him *if* his name stands simply for 'finality' (my-sheaf-stood-in-the-centre). But no one can obstruct the way of the mocked and spat-upon Lord. The spat-upon Lord is the universal Lord! No situation can frighten him.

'Now the tax collectors and sinners were all drawing near to hear him. And the Pharisees and the scribes murmured, saying, "This man receives sinners and eats with them"' (Luke 15.1,2). He reveals his own kind of 'finality' as he 'eats with them'. Should we establish his finality by way of comparison? By way of some theological proofs? It is not our business to establish his finality for him. 'For who has known the mind of the Lord, or who has been his counsellor?' (Rom. 11.34). We are caught by the power of the living Lord. Our foundation of faith is infinitely more secure since we have not laid it. The spat-upon finality is the crucified finality. In his suffering finality (cross) we find the possibility of our life renewed and resurrected. It has come to us! We have not created it! No handle on the cross!

Ian M. Fraser · *The Character of Ministry*

Ian M. Fraser, *The Fire Runs*, SCM Press 1975, pp.112–16

If the people of God keep their nerve, hierarchies have had their day. Bureaucracies which fulfil much the same role attend the same fate. The people of God have come of age. They must fulfil their responsibilities as adults, and reject every form of church government which would keep them children. The hierarchical type of organization belongs to the time of ignorance which God winked at. Now he calls on all men to repent.

Of course there are hierarchies and hierarchies. Are there some which effectively release the people of God into their joyful task? The shape of ministry in the Orthodox churches must be taken with new seriousness as a possible resource – although the service of the hierarchy in releasing the full potential of the people of God is not so obvious to outsiders as it seems to be to Orthodox hierarchies themselves! The point remains – if the people of God are *released* by a form of leadership we are no longer justified in calling that a hierarchy. For hierarchy indicates a sacred caste group who bear rule over others and make decisions for them. Among the defects which attend the hierarchical system of government are these:

(*a*) Their very structures encourage them to become, almost inevitably, 'instead of' organizations. They have a separate identity and prestige. This offers the possibility of acting 'for the good of' others, rather than with them.

(*b*) They are power-groups. They are wide open to the abuse of power to protect their own interests and their own positions. Wherever you find hierarchies you find manipulation, restrictive practices, administrative and financial pressures. They can isolate and relocate disturbers of their peace to defuse 'dangerous' situations. One must, however, go on to ask what kind of power they hold and exercise. Only in a limited number of instances is it brute secular power (an estimate from a reliable source places the capital invested by the Roman Catholic Church in Italian industry at one third of the total). The most dominating institutional church leadership has no apparatus which is the equivalent today of the Inquisition, no contemporary machinery to be compared with police terror and torture. There is always space which people of courage can use if they screw their courage to the sticking point. The problem of the power exercised is rather the attempted control of initiatives or the requirement that initiatives be referred for clearance – a power of the keys, to open things out or shut things down. In Britain, perhaps in Europe, the sins of politeness and diffidence have very often allowed the ordained leadership unilaterally to block or encourage promising developments (the appointment of one unsympathetic bishop effectively took the dynamic out of the Sheffield Industrial Mission).

(*c*) They are male and cannot represent the church.

(*d*) They seem to be constitutionally quite incapable of taking a John the Baptist attitude to new, emerging leadership: '. . . as he grows greater, I must grow less' (John 3.30). Their general characteristic is to inhibit, not to free into service the emerging qualities and gifts of the whole people of God.

This is not true everywhere. Bishop Ah Mya from Rangoon said in a message to his people: 'In the newly-born province of Burma, what we need most is leadership. We need leaders who possess the quality and secret of teamwork, leaders who can quickly spot forces that are good and positive and can mobilize them for the whole Province. Not leaders who feel that they must lead, but leaders who feel that they must so serve as to produce leaders.' In an interview, Pope Shenouda of the Coptic Orthodox Church remarked: 'Authority in the church is a form of the exercise of love, trust and simplicity . . . in any gathering of Christians, truth must preside, not status: then clergy and laity can each exercise their proper authority.' It cannot be said, over the piece, looking back on history, that hierarchies have shown any great capacity 'so to serve as to produce leaders'. Emerging leadership has rarely been something to be welcomed. Rather it has been a threat to magisterial authority; or it has been regarded as presenting an area of confusion and untidiness in the church which would be better to be sorted out and regulated from the top. There is still enough space in most churches for alternative leadership to emerge and make impact. But if the leadership at 'the top' exists to encourage the development of multiple leadership at the base, then hierarchies seem to be quite the wrong instrument.

(*e*) The death seal set on hierarchies is in their non-disposable character. Over the centuries they have assumed a divine validation in themselves – which means that they are not subject to the mind of the people of God when their inadequacies cry out for remedy. They leave enough space to be bypassed, and that is happening all over the world, especially where latinized rather than eastern forms of hierarchies exist. But one must ask whether it is good enough that the overt leadership of the church be set aside or disregarded in order that the covert leadership might help the church to get on with the job. Signs of the times point the need for a leadership which can keep step with the maturing church.

(*f*) The main charge against hierarchies must be that they cannot do what the church needs, to grow up and move outward in love. The habit of trying to make decisions at the top and then filter them down is endemic. Mission cannot start from the top any more than a plant can grow from the flower down.

The action of a man like Dom Helder Camara and his leadership in the hierarchy in the Recife area of Brazil may offer fresh encouragement for the future of this form of church government. But he and those who join with him still form only a very small and unrepresentative proportion of the official leadership in Brazil. A few swallows do not make a summer.

Yet – if everything that is well-rooted starts from the ground, why talk about the need for leadership at all? Cannot God be trusted to raise up whom he chooses, as he raised up the judges in the Old Testament, to provide the kind of leadership that each situation requires? The judges themselves illustrate the weakness of *ad hoc* leadership. By the time we come to the New Testament, it is clear that God has made a more solid and continuous provision for building up his church. But does this mean some body which can act as a power in itself?

The search must be on continually for structures which release the Christian community into movement instead of impeding that community. The only authority which is likely to be acceptable at all today is authority which can authenticate itself as fulfilling a necessary part in forwarding the work of God in the world. Does the Bible give clues about 'releasing structures of ministry' and 'liberating forms of authority'?

Biblically, the word used for matters like 'church order', 'ordination' is a word of deployment.

The ascension of Jesus Christ was not a handover to consecrated men and women. It was the breaking out from its geographical restriction of the ministry Christ once exercised in the incarnation, to the ends of the earth and the end of time. The work of ministry or service is undertaken by Christ alive in the world; and ministry on the part of his people is a sharing in his work and an availability for whatever part he allocates. The gifts of the Spirit are distributed among the whole people. They result in ministries some of which are 'emerging' and are relevant for limited periods, some of which are 'continuing'. The evidence of the New Testament is sometimes dismissed as being too varied and contradictory to give guidance regarding the ordering of ministry today. I believe it to be determinative. It is there quite clear that those who are chosen by God for particular assignments and have this recognized by the Christian community are set apart *for as long as a particular job is committed to them.* It is often not at all clear at the beginning whether the assignment is short-term or long-term – it may be for a large missionary journey, or just the next stage of a journey, or for something like a lifelong parish ministry. No basis can be found for the 'indelible laundry mark' theory – that once the sign is on you it is on you for life. You will not know, when you are set aside, nor will the church know at that point, in what way the commitment to play a particular part in God's overall strategy will work out.

We come back to the biblical basis. The Greek word is a word for the flexible undertaking of an assignment. Taken into a full Christian context, it points to the battles which have to be fought at different points in history by those who are concerned for the coming of the kingdom. It is a word for the march through life of people alert for the engagement of the enemy at any point. When the need for engagement appears, forces break from line of march to be deployed in line of battle. That is what church order is – the deployment of the whole church so that it may be engaged where it matters.

Words for setting apart, ordination, order, etc., are in the first instance words which apply to the whole church. The community of faith has to be where it matters, at the right time to bring its impact to bear; and its forces need to be so disposed as to have maximum effect. Leadership exists to subserve this goal. The work of leadership is to enable the Christian community to serve effectively.

Two sets of questions may highlight a difference which underlines different concepts of leadership:

Here is one set. How is the enemy deployed? What dispositions do we require to contain his thrusts, anticipate his strategy and make a breakthrough? Where should the main troop concentrations be? Who will make a good commander for this or that part of the field in this particular engagement?

Here is another set. Is the pattern of deployment in the best classical tradition? Who should give and who should receive orders? What eminences should be occupied by commanders?

Church leadership had no role except to facilitate the fighting of battles which God wants fought.

Then, coming down to earth, what alternative do we have to hierarchies or bureaucratistic equivalents? What alternative pattern is desirable?

There is no one alternative pattern. Patterns are developing all over the world. We are back in times like those of the early church. The volcanic fires of the gospel are changing out of recognition what were familiar ecclesiastical landscapes. The most obvious thing is what is not being given attention – we must sit at the feet of the world church and discover how God *is* disposing his forces.

Wherever there are areas of freedom, and the church is in movement, varieties of ministry are being worked out which provide pointers. It is a time to discern what forms of ministry are meeting the challenge of the new age so that the whole church can reshape its life – always with the understanding that ministry is likely to be different in different parts of the world just as it has been different at different points of history. Even within one situation, we must be prepared for differences.

A member of ZOTO, the people's organization in Tondo, the shanty settlement in Manila, was asked about leadership in that large community. He replied: 'We make sure that old leaders are quickly discarded if they begin to feel too secure and sure of themselves. We must always be encouraging new leadership to emerge and giving these new people the opportunity to develop skills. We believe that a whole community can take charge of its own destiny – it does not need a small, specially trained and skilled group on whom it must depend year after year. That way you only get power blocs and prevent genuine leadership from emerging.'

Ministry is service within the people of God which ensures space for the working of the Holy Spirit, so that the gifts he gives his people might be recognized and nourished, and so that the many ministries of the whole Christian community might be brought into play. God chooses to extend his blessing, to restore and renew his world, largely through human agents and agencies. Ministry is a means whereby he deploys the resources of all his people so that the world is blessed. Ministry is thus directed to concrete change affecting the whole fabric of society and of personal life – although in some restricted and constricting circumstances, the scale on which this can happen will be limited.

Alternative forms of ministry are sprouting everywhere in the world church. But there is scarcely any desire, in my experience, for a new Protestantism, for an Alternative Church. The historical failure of splits, like that of the Reformation, lies before our eyes, and gives warnings which are being heeded. So there is still time for the meeting, on an equal footing, of the traditional and emerging leadership to discern authentic ways of ministry for the world church. This is now needed, and opportunities to bring it about must be urgently seized.

6 · Spirituality in Politics

It is a common experience to serve on a committee, the members of which hold a variety of religious or ideological positions – or no particular position at all on such matters. Committees on issues from nuclear disarmament to local vandalism function because the members have enough in common to work together on practical matters. In the course of the meeting or during the coffee break there may be good-natured references to more divisive matters on which they are not agreed. It might seem that 'spirituality' would be one such. We need a good autumn day for the rally: perhaps the religious colleagues would see what they can do about that. Nudge, nudge and weak smile. George Macleod tells a story of one of his clerical forbears, a man also of imposing stature, who with a smaller minister colleague had to be taken across to an island by the ferryman. The weather blew up midway and the ferryman's judgment was: 'The little one prays, but the big one rows.'

In these examples we see a distortion and an unfortunate reduction in the meaning of spirituality. It has about it connotations of inability to cope with life, having to be bailed out (literally in the latter case). Curiously, this is quite the opposite of what we mean by 'the spirit of man'. When we say of someone that his captors could not break his spirit we are suggesting that there is something at the very heart of human existence which gives it its peculiar character and value. If the captors did break his spirit the implication is that the broken man would no longer be himself, perhaps that he would no longer be a man at all. This way of speaking is not peculiar to religion. Indeed and unfortunately it is not religious: unfortunate in the sense that religion tends to frown on the suggestion that there is inner strength within man. In different ways Christian theology tends to replace this with the grace of God. But if there is confusion here I think we might be guided by the understanding shared by non-religious people, that the spirit of man is the essential element in human nature that characterizes man.

The example of such spirit which springs to mind is of George Jackson, one of the three 'Soledad Brothers'. When he was eighteen he was sentenced from one-year-to-life for stealing $70 from a petrol station. By American standards it was not a serious crime and his part in it was peripheral. He might reasonably have expected an early parole. But before he met his death, in mysterious circumstances in prison, he had spent ten years in prison, more than seven of them in solitary confinement. It is clear that prison officials thought of him as a bad nigger. If he had been a good one he could have been released at any time. Indeed it is this tragic confrontation which provides us with a fascinating study in the spirit of man. His letters are published under the title *Soledad Brother: The Prison Letters of George Jackson* (Penguin 1971). 'We have a determined enemy who will accept us only on a master-slave basis. When I revolt, slavery dies with me. I refuse to pass it down again. The terms of my existence are founded on that.' And with that his real offence against society comes to light. 'No black will leave this place if he has any violence in his past, until they see that thing in his eyes. And you can't fake it – resignation, defeat – it must be clearly stamped across the face.' Death awaits him. Either George Jackson dies in order to become the kind of being who can be returned to society or he must be locked up till Jackson the man is killed in prison. 'Although I would very much like to get out of here in order to develop a few ideas that have occurred to me – although I would not like to leave my bones here on the hill, if it is a choice between that and surrendering the things that make me a man, the things that allow me to hold my head erect and unbowed, then the hill can have my bones. Many times in the history of our past – I speak of the African here in the US – many times we were presented with this choice, too many times, too many of us choose to live the crippled existence of the near-man, the half-man. Well, I don't care how long I live. Over this I have no control, but I do care about what kind of life I live, and I can control this. I may not live but another five minutes, but it will be five minutes definitely on my terms.'

Here is the paradox of freedom. How is it that a man who is locked up in prison for the rest of his life can be a free man? How is it that one who is hidden away in solitary confinement year after year can be beyond the reach of his captors? In this the true spirit of man is revealed. Spirituality concerns this impenetrable depth of the soul – and spirituality concerns the ways in which the spirit of man is purified and strengthened. As already noted, spirituality in this sense is not an exclusively religious matter, and unfortunately religion has sometimes weakened the spirit of man. George Jackson himself experienced religion as one of those things 'that lock the mind and hinder thinking'. It can, as Marx noted, cloud the imagination and weaken the will to resist. In this sense some forms of religious devotion must be accounted as anti-spiritual. Spiritual things are not for the coffee break but are the very substance of the central issues of human existence, individual and social. Of Herbert Marcuse, the inspiration of many young revolutionaries in Europe and America around 1967, Thomas Merton, Trappist monk said, 'I regard him as a kind of monastic thinker.' And a young revolutionary from Europe responded 'We are monks also', with the implication that the revolutionaries are the *true* monks. The terminology is not decisive, but what is at stake is not who is a monk, but who is a spiritual man, who understands about spiritual things.

We should not too quickly discount the spirituality in man, since according to a Genesis meditation on the nature of man, human life – as distinct from biological existence – owes its origin to man receiving the Spirit of God. There is a traditional spirituality which leads away from an evil world. Today we look for a spirituality that preserves the faithful in the midst of such a world and gathers strength for the long haul. 'Spiritual direction' today might well be guidance for such witness. To many it will seem inappropriate, to some offensive, but the paradox of freedom in the spirituality of George Jackson recalls the spirituality of Gethsemane-and-Calvary: the Man who is free even when in the grasp of his captors, who would not have been more free if his Father had sent 'more than twelve legions of angels'.

It is one of the dangers of liberation theology to assume that liberation is to be measured in the ending of political or economic constraints. Such goals are worthy but in the examples just given we see that they are apparently not ultimate. They are not the final criterion of what makes a man and keeps him human. If they were then generation after generation would be condemned to despair, for in history the constraints are seldom thrown off. Exodus is a constant theme in liberation theology but it is quite unrealistic. Christian faith is not based on Exodus but on that more subtle combination of Calvary-and-Easter. Who would not passionately desire to be released from prison? Who would not passionately pray that this cup should pass away? Of course no leader who has a reputation is going to speak in this way. It is Exodus or nothing. Well, for most of Jewish history it was nothing, they were captive. That has to be said: there is no spirituality here.

Short of the coming of the Kingdom or some secular utopia, the identification of freedom with the end of constraints will always lead to despair. At the risk of being accused of quietism ('nevertheless not as I will, but as thou wilt') let us at least consider that Christian faith is much more profound, that the precursor of Calvary-and-Easter is not Exodus but rather the fiery furnace-and-victory: 'and He *will* deliver us out of your hand, O king. *But if not*, be it known to you, O king ...' This is the spirituality which longs for freedom but is neither taken in by the semblance of it nor defeated in the absence of it.

Tissa Balasuriya · *Spirituality in the Context of Social Justice*

From 'Towards a Spirituality of Social Justice' by Tissa Balasuriya, o.m.i., Director, Centre for Society and Religion, 281 Deans Road, Colombo 10, Sri Lanka. Used by permission of the author

Traditional spirituality conceived of a person's growth in sanctity and union with God as one which led to a life of quiet and withdrawn from the world. If it was active it was to be in the direction of works of mercy, of evangelism or administration of religious or ecclesiastical communities. There has been little reflection on the relationship of sanctity to the conflicts that may arise due to a desire to serve one's neighbour in the direction of justice. This has been the main trend of spirituality specially in the last two centuries when Christians were in dominant positions almost everywhere in the world and the centuries as establishments were in favour of the status quo.

As we move towards action for justice there is a necessary element of conflict, for justice cannot be achieved without fundamental changes, in our society in favour of the oppressed. When such changes are proposed there is naturally opposition of those who would be the losers economically and socially. The forces of defence of the status quo normally hit back with all the means at their disposal; for generally human beings do not give up power till they are compelled to do so by a superior power. Hence conflicts are inevitable in the struggle for justice. It may well be that the issues are also not always one sided. There may be a certain extent of justice in the claims of both sides. Our choices are bound to be ambiguous for we deal in an area in which there is no absolute certainty as in Mathematics.

It is therefore necessary that the action for justice include conflict, contestation and risk bearing. It is within these that we have to articulate a spirituality in which love is the motivation. It is precisely the love for the oppressed which should make us strong in our action against oppression without being bitter against any person.

In this process it is likely that we have to rethink our alliances, friendships and relationships. We may find that groups and persons with whom we have worked for many years are in fact obstacles to social justice. We may even come to the conclusion that persons and institutions that claim to represent God and religion may in fact be strong defenders of the social injustice. Sometimes conflict may come closer home; even the relationships within the family may be strained due to such options. These may cause certain inner tensions within oneself. We may feel alienated from former friends, from entire institutions and perhaps from a special class. The oppressed themselves sometimes do not support persons who want changes for they may be more influenced by the thought conditioning to which they have been subjected during long periods.

We may also find that the forces of law and order, be they the police and military or the religious agencies of moral discipline, may be ranged against our efforts. We have to expect to be challenged in our convictions, attacked in our reputation, and impugned concerning our morality. Our own mental equilibrium may be questioned. We are likely to be isolated, mistrusted, misunderstood calumniated and alienated by many who think they are normal, equilibrated, law-abiding and holy.

On the other hand there may be the conviction that unless we take strong steps to contest the present situation in favour of justice the prevailing unjust order will be strengthened and perpetuated. Hence one's own conscience cannot promote, even if one has to conform to the existing situation in which the oppressed and under-privileged of different categories are compelled to suffer. We need therefore to develop a spirituality in which conflict and contestations are seen as part of the process of growth in self-realization in service of neighbour and of the love of God.

It is precisely such a spirituality which Jesus Christ has borne witness to, for, his public life was one in which he was constantly involved in tensions and conflicts against all the injustices of the society of the day. The height of his agony was on the night before his death when he prayed in the Garden of Olives that this chalice if possible, be taken away from him. His obedience was not to human wisdom or to a constituted authority which could give a sense of security in conformism, but to his own conscience and the will of the Father made manifest through events of his life in that environment. Within these conflicts and tensions he had a deep sense of peace at the profoundest level of his being because he had the conviction that he was doing what he deemed right in love and justice.

The spirituality of social justice can achieve deep interior peace in the midst of conflict and tension; for this we require much reflection and group evaluation in the midst of action. Such a reflection would be quite different from a meditation that is cut off from the struggles and tensions of the day. It is possible even within monastic life as shown by Thomas Merton. But Merton was an exceptional monk who from the interior of his monastery participated in the struggles of our time and that on the side of the oppressed.

Hence a spirituality of social justice has to evolve radical forms of reflection and meditation, prayer and 'retreats.' These will have to include an awareness of the social environment and the options explicit or implicit of a group or person. Prayerful reflection will also require self-criticism and evaluation by the individual and the group for there is always a temptation for us to make comfortable compromises with the existing power structure rather than to keep moving forward towards the promised land in truth and justice. Evaluation, self-criticism and reflection may themselves be part of the tension and conflict, for we may find differences of opinion even among similarly motivated groups. It's not one's sincerity alone that gives meaningfulness to one's commitment, for this has to be tested within a given social context.

In this connection the methodology of spiritual reflections or 'retreats' needs to be recast. The traditional 'retreats' with silence and without reference to socio-political analysis cannot meet the demands of the more radically committed or even socially critical persons and groups. These will need the incorporation of social and group analysis within the perspective of spiritual reflection. Such revaluation of one's life is more difficult and more challenging. It will require also a better long term and immediate preparation. Data gathering regarding social issues and trends and honesty concerning our own options, fears and inhibitions will be material for common reflection. The group in 'retreat' will have to emerge from the exercise with a clearer understanding (and hopefully consensus) on goals, short term objectives, strategies and perhaps even tactics. Presently traditional Christian religious life and spiritual retreats have not yet responded to this need. This is one of the causes for the giving up of the traditional 'retreats' – specially by the younger persons and groups . . .

The evaluation of one's activities along with a group with which one is connected is an important stage in the spirituality of social justice. This is different from the earlier modes of spiritual direction and 'particular examination' in traditional spiritualism. Then spirituality was regarded more or less as a highly individual and almost secret matter. At most there would be a connection between a person and a spiritual director who would give judgement or who would advise according to the dirigee's dispositions. The spirituality then was more one's relationship directly to God without much consideration for social causes. Group evaluation regarding justice is extremely important for several factors such as the determination of goals, the choice of methods, continuing assessment of results, changing one's priorities, options, methods, formation and alliances. It can be a safeguard against individualism, or compromises due to fear, insularity, personal worries, etc. Group evaluation can contribute also to the rounding of temperaments, the accepting of diversities, the pooling of talents, skills, age groups and strategies as well as to giving practicality to prophecy . . .

The growth in social justice is not a mere external phenomenon. It is linked to the refinement of a person's spirit. Traditionalists tend to think that social activism cannot be harmonised with spiritual growth. This is one of the myths of social reaction.

Active commitment to justice may take a person away from the regularity of religious life, or wean him from the devotionalism of the 'pious faithful.' But the very process of social commitment with its risks, tensions, conflicts and ruptures is not likely to take place without deep reflection. It requires a more thoughtful decision for a person to commit himself to the defence of civil rights in a time of political repression than to lie low and meditate in a convent chapel or attend a weekly novena. Profound reflection is required for motivation, action and evaluation. This is true for all – be they persons of a religious persuasion or otherwise. Marx, Lenin, Mao Tse Tung and Mahatma Ghandi were all men of deep reflection while being passionately committed to action for justice.

For the Christian the prayer of social justice can find substance in the scriptures, specially in the life and teaching of Christ. The prayer he taught, the 'Our Father', is intimately connected with social justice. 'Give us today our daily bread'.... 'Thy kingdom come on earth as in heaven' are eminently related to the concerns of justice. To call God 'Father' of all is to take an option against all forms of social discrimination based on race, class, caste and sex.

Such a contemplation places the axe of self purification on our whole social being. It affects our choice of work and employment. Thus those who opt out of an exploiting system to try to change by contesting it are in fact expressing in the reality of their lives the meaning of the call to love God and neighbour. Spirituality has to appreciate what is going on in the mind, heart and will of so many who make such options.

Unfortunately traditional spirituality has hardly any place for it – at least not in the categories of the spiritual and mystical theology of the 19th and the first half of this century. The extent to which Christianity has been conditioned by the prevailing social system is so deep that even mystical theology has been confined within the limit of the status quo. This is one reason why so many radicals specially youth find the traditional religious approach unhelpful to them – and even an obstacle to the self understanding of their noblest inspirations and motivations.

Social justice is one of the principal concerns of the more generous youth of our time. When they discover the radical call of Christ, they are happy and motivated to greater generosity. Often times they have to contest the existing values, practices and regulations of the Church to experience an authentic relationship of justice and love in their action and prayer. The contestation concerning the Eucharist is an example of such a search. A work like Daniel Berrigan's 'Dark Night of Resistance' can help us rediscover the radical meaning of the gospel and of the following of Christ in our times.

As one grows in one's commitment to justice one is bound to suffer in different forms – physically, psychologically and socially. This can be mingled with the joy of suffering for a cause. This is one of the processes of self purification that can lead to greater union with God. It has also to be linked to a love of persons that avoids all hatred and bitterness and a service to those in need. The virtue of social justice can help to bring about a harmony between one's subjective motivations and the objective requirements of the kingdom of God. Then personal sanctity will have a more creative impact on the world outside ourselves. This form of contemplation may be said to be at least as truly God centered as the traditional passive contemplation.

It is a pity that traditional Christian spirituality did not evaluate contemplation and mysticism in relation to its impact on society. Perhaps in past times this was not in the public consciousness. But today it cannot be avoided with good faith. Contemplation of God to be objectively authentic must relate to the struggle for the building of the kingdom of God on Earth. Otherwise it will be objectively counter productive – even if subjectively well intentioned.

If and when religions understand the radical and revolutionary demands of their basic message – they will cease to be obstacles to justice. At that stage the temples and Churches will not be frequented merely for personal favours within social conservatism. Then there will be a conflict between the exploitative social system and institutionalized religion. It will then be seen how close the love of God is to the dedicated service of man and the struggle for a better world. For such an approximation to take place, the spirituality of social justice needs to be evolved in actual life experience by committed persons, groups and Churches.

Action for justice implies a dying to self in one's possessions, values, and relationships. In Asia today, where repression is on the increase, a person committed to social justice will have to suffer much. It may result in loss of status and employment, even imprisonment, and separation from one's dearest companions in life. Ultimately in the moment of deep suffering one is alone. On the cross Jesus was alone. It was also his supreme moment of self giving in love. The quest for justice can lead to a self donation in which love can experience existentially the price and joy of love. This love is not mere sentimentality or paternalism. It is experienced in one's flesh and blood. It may be a profound form of self purifying contemplative union with God in love of others.

José Miguez Bonino · *Red Heroes and Christian Martyrs*

José Miguez Bonino, *Christians and Marxists*, Hodder & Stoughton 1976, pp.133–36, 139–42

With some of our considerations in the last chapter we have already moved into a dimension which is not easily subject to analytic thought: the level of attitudes, stances, approaches to life which I will call, risking a broad and ambiguous word, 'spirituality'. Spirituality, in this sense, is a total way of life which grows out of and surrounds any deep commitment. It is the projection of a total engagement on everything that a man thinks, does, dreams. As such, it is not an exclusively Christian phenomenon. We find it wherever we meet deep commitment, because deep commitments are total: they affect all aspects of life and subordinate everything to them. They make a total claim. Such is, of course, the stuff of both heroism and fanaticism. J. B. S. Haldane said that fanaticism is one of the only four important inventions made between 3000 BC and AD 1400. And Eric Hoffer comments: 'It was a Judaic-Christian invention. And it is strange to think that in receiving this malady of the soul the world also received a miraculous instrument for raising societies and nations from the dead – an instrument of resurrection.'

Whether total commitment to a cause is a malady or the only possibility of human health can, of course, be debated. Christianity and Marxism share the view that the latter is the case, however they may differ in their understanding of the nature and demands of this commitment. No honest observer will, in effect, deny that communism has developed a total commitment and a deep 'spirituality' in the sense we are using this word. Like all deep spiritualities, it becomes particularly visible and moving in relation to the frontiers of human life, the critical points: love, solitude, suffering, death. We cannot leave our consideration of the relation of Christians and Marxists within a revolutionary process without touching – however briefly – on the question of spirituality.

Communist heroes

What we have called spirituality can be roughly translated in Marxist terms by the notion of 'militancy'. To begin on the negative side, I may comment on the deep impression made on me by reading the biography of Josef Stalin by the – deeply opposed – Trotskyist Isaac Deutscher. Here is a person who can scarcely evoke spontaneous sympathy. He acts sometimes out of obscure and even inhuman motivations. Callousness, hatred, cynicism appear quite frequently in his words and actions. He will grasp for power and use it unashamedly. He will destroy, bend, overpower. He can be ruthless and cold. But one feels always in the presence of a man who, in his innermost being, has given himself to a cause, which is not always very clear and well defined (and therefore quite frequently turned into his own whim), but which masters his whole life. There is no frivolity, no equivocation, no possible relativising of this commitment. Whatever else he may be, he is – subjectively – a 'militant'.

I have chosen a rather perverse example, because it seems to me to indicate that communism, even at its worst, displays a depth which we cannot ignore. There is a seriousness which reminds us of the Puritan concentration on 'the one thing that matters', the exclusion of all that is superfluous or distracting in terms of the one purpose and goal. There is a total subordination of subjectivity and subjective feeling: love, family, artistic or emotional satisfaction, even one's own life and security – everything is 'counted as loss' for the sake of the cause. Sometimes we shudder at the ruthlessness of this total concentration. It is for us difficult to understand how a proud and intelligent Soviet theorist – like the ones who died under Stalin – will 'confess his mistakes' – obviously unreal – before the party, not in order to escape punishment, but because he knows that, in the long run, and in spite of himself, the party is right because the future belongs to it. Party discipline is not, for the militant, an external imposition: it is the core of his spirituality. However repulsive the manifestations of this total devotion may be, we have to respect them and to recognise that they have also appeared – both in their sublime and in their repugnant forms – at the crucial and most decisive points in the history of Christian spirituality. There is a hairbreadth line between fanaticism and devotion. Communism and Christianity have often illustrated both to a unique degree.

We could, of course, find innumerable examples of heroic and selfless devotion among Marxists. One thinks of the Italian hero Antonio Gramsci, living his death in Mussolini's prison and concentrating his last ounces of strength and lucidity to the cause of the proletariat of his country, without bitterness, totally consecrated to a future which he would not see. Or one can think of Ernesto (Ché) Guevara, forsaking his well-earned place of privilege and power in the triumphant Cuban revolution to risk his life every day in the Bolivian jungle. Ernst Bloch has celebrated the communist willingess to lay down their life in his epic of the 'red hero', the men who were killed for their opposition to Hitler in the concentration camps of Nazi Germany. His words are worth quoting because they reflect the depth and character of this total surrender:

> All those who are sacrificed take to the tomb the flowers of yesterday, some of which are withered and unrecognisable. Only one category of man advances towards death almost totally dispossessed of all traditional consolation: he is the red hero. He confesses up to his death the cause for which he has lived and clearly, coldly, consciously, he advances towards that Nothingness in which he has learned to believe as a free spirit. His sacrifice is different from that of the ancient martyrs: these died almost without an exception with a prayer on their lips, confident that they had thus merited Heaven ... But the Communist hero, whether under the Tsars, under Hitler or under any other power, sacrifices himself without hope of resurrection. His Good Friday is not sweetened – much less absorbed – by any Easter Sunday, a Sunday in which he will personally return to life. The Heaven to which the martyrs raised their arms amidst flames and smoke, does not exist for the red materialist. And nevertheless he dies confessing a cause, and his superiority can only be compared with that of the very early Christians or of John the Baptist.

Nobody who is acquainted with the tortures, the suffering, the death of thousands of communist revolutionaries – as we are today in Latin America – will want to retract or relativise a single word of this moving homage. 'Greater love has no man than this, that a man lay down his life for his friends' (John 15:13).

Christian martyrs

The Christian who enters the revolutionary struggle does not set up his spirituality over against the Marxist as if it were a contest. He will simply live out his faith as loyally and confidently as he can, with the help of the Holy Spirit. It is not, therefore, my intention, to compare Christian and communist spirituality, but to indicate what seems to me basic for a Christian spirituality within the struggle for human liberation. Again, these are only very simple and initial lines – only real life will develop them.

To be a believer means to participate in the movement of love which brough Jesus Christ to share our human life, emptying himself of his power and glory and assuming the fragility, the temptation and even the guilt of man, giving his own life even unto the death of the cross. What is here at stake is not a mere 'imitation' but a participation in the lot of solidary love, the only thing that can really create a possibility of new life for man. For this reason, the Apostle Paul does not hesitate in referring to his own suffering – physical as well as spiritual – as his participation in 'what still has to be fulfilled in the sufferings of Christ'. It is not that Christ left something undone, but that he opened for us a way of serving men in which the disciple enters now, paying the price or, as Jesus himself said, 'taking up his cross'.

Not every suffering has this character: it is that suffering which results from taking in love responsibility for others: 'nobody has a greater love than this, that he may give his life for his friends', or, as Paul comments, for those whom he loves, even though they may still consider themselves his enemies. It is the inevitable suffering that comes with service. Why? Because we live in a world which has turned its back to love, the world of injustice, the world which accepts the norms of the anti-Kingdom. Whoever undertakes (whether Christian or not) to introduce that which corresponds to true humanity, justice and peace, has final reality on his side, but the present structure of the world (for us, at present, very concretely as a capitalist order!) against him. The old world resents his presence and tries to eliminate him. Sometimes it succeeds – and then his solidarity with Christ is fulfilled: he 'witnesses .. unto blood'.

We must try to understand carefully what is here in question. It is not the masochism which finds satisfaction in suffering or rejection. To be a disciple is, in Christian terms, to enlist in a conflict which is still raging, however much its outcome may be evident to faith. To share the lot of the Captain, to be found 'worthy of suffering for Christ and with him', to place body and soul side by side with him – and (with him) with those for whom he came – is the greatest joy of the soldier. To share in the victory, to participate in the triumphal procession, is not an isolated privilege that one 'buys' through suffering: it is part of that very same participation, of having become one – rather, having been made one – with the Lord. And victory and celebration are the triumph of love, the consummation of the Kingdom on which the hope of all – the victor and the defeated – hangs equally. The triumph of God is the welfare of men. For this the Christian will be glad to pay the price.

Be glad: in faith and hope, the final victory is already present.

And therefore tragedy, suffering and death do not have the final word. The Brazilian theologian Rubem Alves has very acutely underlined 'the political significance of the Sabbath': it is the day that represents 'the politics of God', the fact that, beyond our toil and effort, our commitment and seriousness, our concern and responsibility, lies the certainty of God's own promise. We do not carry the burden of the whole world on our back, we carry only the burden of the day. We can rest! God himself can rest and simply enjoy the praise of creation because the 'goodness' of his work, however compromised in the struggle, cannot be undone. And we can rest – we can pray, and play, and love, and laugh – in the midst of toil. Therefore, there is nothing contradictory, but quite to the contrary, the deepest secret and ethos of Christian spirituality, in Paul's paradoxical exhortation: 'Rejoice in suffering!'

I cannot but feel that there is a deep and fundamental lack in Marxist philosophy at this point; an impossibility to make sense of the experience of joy, personal fulfilment, hope and love which many of the militants have so beautifully illustrated. The very life of Marx is full of a deep compassion, a sensitivity to friendship and joy, a love of beauty, which finds little place in his view of man as a mere 'determinate species-being'. I cannot refrain from quoting from a letter written in 1856 (the year in which he was deeply involved in working for *Das Kapital*) to his 'dearest darling' (his wife):

> But love – not of Feuerbachian man, not of Moleschott's metabolisms, not of the proletariat, but love of one's darling, namely you, *makes a man into a man again*. In fact there are many women in the world, and some of them are beautiful. But where can I find another face in which every trait, even every wrinkle brings back the greatest and sweetest memories of my life? Even my infinite sorrows, my irreplaceable losses I can read on your sweet countenance, and I kiss my sorrows away when I kiss your sweet face. 'Buried in your arms, awoken by your kisses' – that is, in your arms and by your kisses, and the Brahmins and Pythagoreans can keep their doctrine of reincarnation and Christianity its doctrine of resurrection.

This is not merely the new 'social man' which a change in the mode of production can create (although a competitive and inhuman mode of production can deprive man, and does deprive many a man, of the possibility of experiencing and bringing to consciousness this love). This is a testimony of a humanity that roots deeper than the commitment to a human cause. How can this human experience

– and many another that could be mentioned – be seen, and lived, not as a distraction from commitment, not as a substitute for responsibility, but in a unity and integrity in which it reinforces, gives depth and meaning to the struggle?

These last pages are not an attempt to extol Christian spirituality as an argument. A Christian knows that faith is not at the end of a syllogism. He will simply offer his witness, not so much in words but in his life. Or rather, in the words that participate in the texture of his life. Such witness is always an invitation, extended in hope and joy, to that kind of life which is for us present and permanent reality, the life in Christ. In the community of human struggle, Christian faith becomes an invitation under the conditions of responsible, joyful solidary militancy.

It is necessary, particularly where we have been dealing with the most 'spiritual' dimensions of Christian life, to remind ourselves that we are still speaking about political and social engagement – we are still in the world of social struggle, economic considerations, political programme, revolutionary theory, perhaps jail and torture, in any case conflict. It is here that the Christian lives his witness. Perhaps some of us will not share the course of action, nor agree with the political and tactical decisions chosen by Néstor Paz, a young Bolivian Christian who joined the guerrillas and died of starvation in the jungle. But I can hardly think of a more appropriate expression of Christian spirituality than the last entry in his diary:

You know, God, that I have tried by all means to be faithful to you ... This is why I am here. I see love as the urgency to solve the problem of the other person, in whom you meet me. I left everything I had and came here. Today is perhaps my Thursday and this night my Friday. I lay everything I am in your hands with a trust that has no limits because I love you ... because you are my Father. No death is useless if the life has been heavy with meaning, and I think this is true of us. Goodbye, Lord; until that Heaven of yours, that new world we desire so much!

José Porfirio Miranda · *Anti-cultus*

José Porfirio Miranda, *Marx and the Bible*, Orbis Books, Maryknoll and SCM Press 1977, pp.53–60, 64–65

To hear or interpret the anticultic invective of the prophets as the oratorical impulse of a well-intentioned preacher whose assertions should be taken with a grain of salt is, in the first place, scientifically unfounded, because the same could be done with the whole Bible and there is no textual reason to prefer the anticultic passages. But second and more important, to interpret in this way is to adopt precisely the hermeneutical position in which understanding becomes impossible. If we consider the prophets to be exaggerating, we suppose ourselves to know Yahweh and revelation better than they. We reserve to ourselves the right to discriminate between what is exaggeration and what is not. And then the Bible really cannot modify our hierarchy of values, which means that it cannot tell us anything new.

With regard to Jesus' criticism of the ritual purifications – 'You put aside the commandment of God to maintain the tradition of men' (Mark 7:8) – Jewish exegete C. G. Montefiore offers his counter-criticism: Jesus does not demonstrate that ritual observance is the cause of their disobedience of God. The Pharisees could have refuted Jesus' statement with a simple 'also,' that is, 'you should do one just as much as the other.' The similarity between this Jewish countercriticism and the customary arguments of Christian morality and dogma is obvious. In 'alsoist' terms, Montefiore is irrefutable, and Jesus is the one who is in error . . .

In this matter if there are those who wish to distinguish between the Old and the New Testaments it is because they have not understood the reason for the anticultus of the prophets. And indeed this is exactly what occurred in the case of Montefiore. If he does not understand the anticultic polemic of Jesus, it is because he has not grasped the reason for the polemic of the prophets. We return to this point because it is here that the difference between the God of the Bible and all the other gods becomes unconcealable.

The customary apologetic argument is that 'the prophets do not condemn cultus as such.' It is thereby deduced that they anathematized only a certain kind of cultus or a certain way of rendering cultus and that they thus tended to reform the cultus or to demand the appropriate internal dispositions. This is how the prophetic anathemas are reduced to pious exhortations of spiritual guidance.

But to know that the prophets did not condemn 'cultus as such' we need not even open the Bible; it is enough to know that they were not Greeks or scholastics. The thesis under consideration has no more to do with the Bible than its opposite: 'The prophets do not approve of cultus as such.' If we decide to look at the Bible the first thing we must establish is that the prophets were quite unconcerned about 'cultus as such.' But we also must establish that it is impossible to reduce their anticultus to a demand for the correct dispositions in the worshipper or a demand for a reform of the cultus or a demand 'to do one just as much as the other.' See Amos 5:21–25:

> I hate and despise your feasts,
> I take no pleasure in your solemn festivals.
> When you offer me holocausts,
> I reject your oblations,
> and refuse to look at your sacrifices of fattened cattle.
> Let me have no more of the din of your chanting,
> no more of your strumming on harps.
> But let right [*mišpaṭ*] flow like a river
> and justice [*ṣᵉdaḳah*] like an unfailing stream.
> Did you bring me sacrifice and oblations in the desert
> for all those forty years, House of Israel?

Here Yahweh does not demand interhuman justice 'besides' cultus; nor does he require that the cultus be reformed; nor is he asking that the cultus be maintained but with better internal dispositions. What he says can be summarized in this way: *I do not want cultus, but rather inter-human justice.* Whatever we do to interpret this message in some other way is pure subterfuge. Nor would it be objective to summarize his message as if he said simply, 'I do not want cultus.' This phrase is inseparable from what follows and what indeed carries the emphasis: *but rather interhuman justice.* This is the very message of Isa. 1:10–20; Hos. 5:1, 2, 6; 6:6; 8:13; Amos 4:4–5; Mic. 6:6–8; Jer. 6:18–21; 7:4–7, 11–15, 21–22; Isa. 43:23–24; 58:2, 6–10. The message is the same whether in the eighth century or in the seventh century or in the postexilic period. I am not going to transcribe these passages; I insist only on one point which is more explicit in Isa. 1:10–20 than in other passages, namely, that prayer is also rejected ... Let it be clearly understood that v. 15, which puts prayer in a list among the most diverse expressions of cultus, excludes the possibility of finding the God of the Bible by means of prayers.

Now is the moment to take up again Montefiore's objection, which is that of all the harmonists of past and present: In what way does cultus hinder the prophets (or Yahweh)? It is very well that they should demand interhuman justice, but there is no reason that they should pose the dilemma between justice and cultus, between prayer-to-God and compassion on the poor.

What is certain is that the prophets do indeed pose this dilemma and with an unavoidable seriousness. In the whole Bible there is no message more serious and central than this, for on it depends our understanding of the difference between the one true God and all the other gods which we men create with our images or philosophies or theologies or religions. The dilemma between justice and cultus occurs because while there is injustice among a people worship and prayer do not have Yahweh as their object even though we have the formal and sincere 'intention' of addressing ourselves to the true God. To know Yahweh is to do justice and compassion and right to the needy. If it were a question of a god accessible through direct knowledge, that is, of a nontranscendent god, there would be no dilemma. The essence of the idol is in this: We can approach it directly. It is entity, it is being itself; it is not the implacable moral imperative of justice.

The objection of naturalism and horizontalism, which should rather be directed in the first place against the entire Bible, passes over the only decisive point of revelation: The question is not whether someone is seeking God or not, but whether he is seeking him where God himself said that he is. This is the point of radical irreconcil-ability between Greek and Western philosophy on the one hand and biblical revelation on the other: 'Ontology, as a fundamental philosophy which does not call into question the self, is a philosophy of injustice' (Levinas). If we are able to prescind from the cry of the poor who seek justice by objectifying God and believing that, because he is being, he is there as always, since being is objective and does not depend on any considerations of our minds nor on what we can or cannot do, at that very moment he is no longer God but an idol. And this is what happened to Christianity from the time it fell into the hands of Greek philosophy. When we demand the dehellenization of Christianity, what we are demanding is that idolatry not be imposed on us, for we do not wish to know any other god than the God of Jesus Christ.

There is an apparently obvious religious objection to the anti-cultus of the prophets: If there can be cultus only when there is justice, then there will never be cultus, for justice will never be realized. But we must in any case make one thing clear: The prophets were convinced that justice would indeed be achieved on earth (and this conviction was shared by Jesus, Paul, John, the Synoptics, the Yahwist, the Deuteronomist, the Priestly tradition, the entire Psalter, and the author of the Letter to the Hebrews). Thus cultus will be acceptable to the prophets at the time when justice has been achieved: Isa. 2:2–4 (cf. Isa. 4, Isa. 32, Isa. 9, and Isa. 11); Mic. 4:1–8; Hos. 14:2–3 (cf. Hos. 2:19–23); Zeph. 3:9–13. Note the grand message of the last part of the book of Ezekiel about the return of the glory of Yahweh to the temple; but this will occur when there are no longer hearts of stone (Ezek. 36:26). Only then – says Yahweh – 'I will be your God.' Note also the burning hopes of Zechariah in relation to the temple; but they will be realized when 'Injustice' (*hariš'ah*) has been torn out from the holy land and carried to the land of *Šin'ar* (Zech. 5:5–11). *It is not a matter of excluding cultus but rather of this very clear message: first justice and then cultus.*

The objection we have been considering reveals a hermeneutical option in the deepest sense, and here Marx does indeed have something to say: Whoever is capable of resigning himself to the fact that justice will never be realized is incapable of taking the prophets seriously. Everything that they wrote, did, and said stems precisely from the fact that they did not resign themselves to injustice. To avoid problems, one can classify as utopian all the hope of the Old and New Testaments and the God who by his very essence originated this hope. But then one would have to hold to a Christ-of-private-faith, for the historical Jesus, Paul, John, and the Synoptics were convinced that the kingdom of God absolutely had to be realized. And on earth, of course.

And finally let us touch on the last objection to the anticultus of the prophets: If the people withdraw from cultus they will have even less hope of learning justice, for it is only contact with God which will teach them justice. As is obvious from what we have been saying, those who put forth this objection have not understood the reason for the anticultus. Basing themselves on the one thing that the Bible has to reveal to us – that is, the difference between Yahweh and the other gods – the prophets deny the entire presupposition of such an objection, namely, that cultus and prayer could put the people in contact with Yahweh while injustice exists on earth. The formal and sincere intention of 'addressing ourselves' to Yahweh while prescinding from the cry of the needy does not make Yahweh accept and value this 'as if' we were addressing ourselves to him when really we are addressing not him, but rather an idol which we decide to call Yahweh. 'When you stretch out your hands, I turn my eyes away. You may multiply your prayers, I shall not listen.... Search for justice, and help the oppressed [or stop the oppressor]; do justice to the orphan, plead for the widow' (Isa. 1:15, 17).

It is precisely this juridical fiction of the 'as if' which Jeremiah combats among the false prophets and priests of the reform undertaken by King Josiah. Jeremiah untiringly calls this reform a 'lie': cf. Jer. 7:4–8, 21–23; 8:8–12; 14:11–16; 23:25–29; etc. The reform of Josiah was as well intentioned as all those undertaken by Christianity in our times. On the one hand it adopted the concern of the eighth-century prophets for the poor, the orphan, and the widow; but on the other, with regard to cultus it did not deem it prudent to wait until justice could be achieved. This is exactly the mentality we find behind the objection which we have been considering. Since it does not understand the difference between Yahweh and the other gods it does not consider that this harmonistic approach gets caught up in a vicious circle. It leads us to believe that we can enter into contact with Yahweh while prescinding from the beseeching cry of the poor and the needy.

The fact seems to me to be today beyond doubt: The eighth-century prophets were no longer around to oppose Josiah's reformism and the superficiality of the priests and scribes, but Jeremiah did understand how all this manifestation of goodwill directly hindered the people from knowing the true nature of the God of Israel. Smend is correct: If Jeremiah rejected the reform of Josiah – for the message of the prophets cannot be accepted through reforms or 'integrations' – 'much less can it be supposed that Amos would have acted differently.' The anticultic polemic of the prophets was 'a battle against the exponents of a false conception of God.' In his detailed analysis Dobbie states that the contrast between the Josianic priests and the prophets goes beyond temperamental or professional animosity. It stems from mutually exclusive conceptions of religion.

What is at the bottom of all this is a different God. And the difference goes far beyond all metaphysical questions. Only thus can we explain the Bible's lack of interest in the problem of whether or not the other gods exist. Such a question moves on the level of being, while the God of the Bible is known in the implacable moral imperative of justice.

What is most significant here is that whether the other gods are entities or not is of no concern to the biblical authors. Otherwise the exegetes would not still be so perplexed by the question. The unique character of the God of Israel is irreducible to ontological questions, no matter how many efforts and analogies the philosophy derived from the Greeks might make in the belief that it can understand everything in terms of being. The Western absolutization of the ontological point of view makes us believe that this instrument of cognition is superior to that of the Bible. But we do not consider how presumptuous and even ridiculous it is to suppose that we know God better than Moses and the prophets did. And, most importantly, we do not consider that it was not because of an ethnologically specific mentality or culture that Israel knew God as it did, but it was rather because of the unconfused specificity of the one true God that a special way of knowing came into existence so that this specificity might be known.

From these passages [I John 4:12, 4:16, 4:20, 4:7–8] it is clear that the direct inaccessibility of God should not be understood as in Greek philosophy, that is, that what is immaterial is unknowable to the sight and to the other senses because they are material, but is knowable to the intellect which is immaterial. John does not reduce himself simply to 'no one has ever seen him,' but rather also affirms that they 'have not *known* God.' John's intention is clearly directed to maintaining that God is knowable only through one's neighbor. It is not enough to say that God is knowable only through transforming revelation, which was the thesis of the gnostics. Unquestionably we are speaking of a God who is God only *in the* revealing of himself, *in the* commanding. But this revelation and command is not direct. It is possible *only through the neighbor who must be loved* (love understood here in the sense we have indicated, that is, love-justice). For John what is in question is not the limitations and defects of our cognitive organs with regard to some object of a category too elevated for them, an object which would be knowable to some superhuman intellect. In John's thesis there is not even a shadow of this epistemological problem. For John the question is rather that God is not God when we try to approach him while avoiding our neighbor. This is precisely the anticultic teaching of the prophets: I do not want cultus, but rather interhuman justice.

Therefore, this is not a revealing that is a transmission of previously unpossessed data or knowledge; this is not a revealing which can be prescinded from, once these data or knowledge are transmitted, as if it were a means which already had achieved its end. Such is the case with Greek science and with all Western sciences without exception, beginning with philosophy and theology, from which the rest historically branched out as if from a trunk. In the Greco-Western approach to knowledge, the other and the others can disappear once they have fulfilled their informative or instructive task. Their contribution is absorbed by the self; it is summarized in and replaced by a representation or an affirmation, made by the self, of the extramental existence of a something. This is a transcendental affirmation of being. This operation is, in any case, an exercise of the self. It involves the disappearance of the radical otherness which, falling under the power of the thinker, loses its resistance as an exterior being. There is truth, I do not deny it: the correspondence between the intellect and the thing. But it is the intellect which possesses this same truth and makes it its own; truth becomes part of the self.

7 · Voices from Asia

Few theologians, wherever they live, are concerned with political theology. But those who are are dealing with the relationship of a religion which has had a profound influence on the development of their culture. What more natural than that they should reflect on the interaction of that religion and the political realities of the culture? So it is in Europe, in the Americas, both North and South. So too even in Black Africa. But when we turn to Asia the situation is altogether different. Other religions have been as influential, often much more influential. Attitudes, values, institutions have not flowed from Christianity – and happily Asian theologians need not take the blame for every religious opiate of the past!

In October 1968, Thomas Merton boarded a plane in San Francisco to begin his trip to Asia. In his *Asian Journal* (Sheldon Press 1974) he records his thoughts. 'We left the ground – I with Christian mantras and a great sense of destiny, of being at last on my true way after years of waiting and wondering and fooling around. May I not come back without having settled the great affair.' Tragically he did not come back. But even he, included in *A Reader in Political Theology* as one who preserved the dialectic of spirituality and political action, did not think of Asia as a place where he would meet Christians. 'I am going home, to the home where I have never been in this body, where I have never been in this washable suit (washed by Sister Gerarda the other day at the Redwoods) ...' No doubt the feminists of chapter 4 would be interested in this division of labour but the homecoming to which he refers is to that continent of monastic contemplation.

Where is political theology in such a continent? What are Christians thinking and doing? Well, many of them are following the example of their fellow Christians in the West and therefore do not engage in political theology or provide material on which we might reflect. Indeed we in the West have much to answer for in this respect. Joseph Comblin underlines the danger elsewhere. 'Any Latin American who has studied in Europe has to undergo detoxification before he can begin to act.' This may well be true of Asia. Gerald Anderson in his collection *Asian Voices in Christian Theology* appends an impressive bibliography of articles, in Western languages. It is divided by country but in each section a high proportion of articles and books are concerned with essentially Western issues, or the issues which missionaries considered to be important in Asia. In the more prestigious journals it is rather depressing to see how Western scholarship is pursued. Fine young graduates are given the opportunity of studying in Europe or the United States and feel constrained on their return to continue to contribute to theological concerns which, if truth be told, are already over-subscribed by Western scholarship. Perhaps the returning Asian theologians feel they will only be taken seriously if they continue such games.

Happily this is not the whole story. There is another kind of Christian thought and practice in Asia of special interest to political theology. For various reasons it is not readily available to Western readers. I take this opportunity of recording my indebtedness to John England for all his help in drawing to my attention many relevant books, articles and statements. I regret that because of the structure of this book I cannot even begin to do justice to the material. However this may support my argument that he really must himself publish a review of the situation in different parts of Asia. But there is an even more ominous reason why the material is not readily available. Not that it is written in local languages, but that it is written under persecution. The creative edge of Christian thinking in Asia is to be found in countries under martial law, in communities intimidated by the state, in prisons and detention camps. Such conditions are not conducive to tomes: testimony precedes treatise. In response to my request for guidance Choan-Seng Song wrote: 'I may be wrong, but my feeling is that in South-East Asia circumstances force us to express our concerns by means of confessing Christian faith.' And certainly there has been a flood of statements by individuals and groups, commenting on particular social and political situations, making their positions clear, identifying themselves although aware of the possible consequences.

To 'choose this day' in such circumstances can have frightening consequences. Father Edicio de la Torre reports such an incident from 1972. 'Most of those involved were nuns, seminarians, ex-seminarians, ministers especially from the Roman Catholic Church. There is no outlet of the normal human energies so they come out for political work. We don't know, a lot of political language is better expressed in sexual terms. I mean the whole analogy of conception, birth, new society. I was even once accused of theological rape, I am serious. A nun vomited because of a four-hour teach-in. I was asking them to commit, to decide. Then I don't know, she vomited, so they accused me of theological rape.' Yet the greater charge must surely be against those who transmit to Asia a theology which mutilates individuals and suggests that the faith is about something other than the realities of life. In many countries the 'confessing church' is in a situation not unlike that of the early church in the Roman Empire. And not surprisingly a recurring theme in Asian political theology concerns the cross and the 'pain of God'. After all, Jesus did not die in bed at a ripe old age, nor was he transported directly to heaven at the first hint of danger. Y. Kim's account of the church in Korea suggests that their suffering has uncovered to them the mystery of the cross more profound than its traditional metaphysical and de-politicized meaning. And it is impossible to read Josef Widyatmadja's article on 'Incarnation as Subversion' without contrasting it with the treatment of the doctrine in *The Myth of God Incarnate* (ed. John Hick, SCM Press 1977). Who understands its Christian significance better? The other selection comes from the 'Theological Writing Collective of the Christians for National Liberation'. One of the poems written by this group tells us that

> There are smaller prisons
> for those who would break down
> bigger and thicker walls
> not to escape
> from the rest
> but to open up the world
> and its future
> to people whose hopes
> have faltered in the dark.

We are fortunate if we have not been so put to the test, but we should do well to listen to the voices from Asia. Perhaps precisely because it is the one continent in which Christianity is not at home it will be the cradle for the rebirth of faith.

Theological Writing Collective · *Mao-Tse-Tung and Filipino Theology*

From 'Red China and the Self-Understanding of the Church', a paper prepared by the Theological Writing Collective of the Christians for National Liberation for an ecumenical colloquium on 'Christian Faith and the Chinese Experience' held in Louvain, September 1974, under the sponsorship of Pro Mundi Vita and the Lutheran World Federation.

The paper was reprinted in *Christianity and the New China* (Ecclesia Publications, Pasadena 1976) and is copyrighted by and reproduced here by permission of the Lutheran World Federation

PERSPECTIVE

Within the context of the present Philippine situation, we accept Marxism-Leninism-Mao-Tse-Tung-Thought (MLMTT) as the most efficacious revolutionary theory – the theory that we believe would guide and lead the national and social liberation movement to victory. This has impelled those of us who consider ourselves Christians to rethink the meaning of our faith and our understanding of the Church, keeping foremost in our minds the reality of oppression, injustice, and class struggle in our society.

It is our conviction that we can no longer rest on the principle that our faith has all the answers to the problems of the given oppressive situation of the people of God in the Philippines, nor can we rely solely in all confidence on the authority of the Church as *mater et magistra* in our impassioned search for solutions to the plight of our people. Yet this is not to deny that the gospel message helps motivate us and gives certain eschatological perspectives in our participation in the liberation movement. The truth remains, however, that the faith has nothing to offer when it comes to defining political lines and programmes, and much less to planning correct strategies and tactics to be employed in the radical restructuring of our society. In addition, we also have to reckon with the fact that, historically, the Christian Church in this country has been grossly identified with service to the ruling classes.

We believe that the Christian religion in the Philippines should now cease to be an opiate of the people. If it is to be authentic, it has to serve the revolution, where it can seek a new birth. Our understanding of the faith and the Church has to find its context in and be shaped by the oppressive reality in our society as analytically viewed by the revolutionary theory of MLMTT. Such understanding, in the final analysis, will in turn serve to enrich and perfect our analysis of the social situation in the perspective of MLMTT. What results, therefore, is a solid grasp of the global situation of our people in the light of our *new* understanding of Christianity and under the guidance of the said revolutionary theory. Again, if our synthetic view of the sad condition of our people is not to degenerate into empty, abstract thought, it should never be frozen and divorced from the concrete process of the liberation struggle.

How does Christianity help us in the struggle? Or is it altogether irrelevant? We are convinced that we cannot waste our time trying to preserve a type of Christianity and an understanding of the Church that have no relation to the liberation of our people. Are we to commit ourselves to these if they too share in the alienation, exploitation, and oppression of the majority of our people? To our mind, it is only too logical that we must subject our understanding of the faith and the Church to serious criticism, if they are to be of real service to our people, who must create their own history and actualize concretely in time their freedom as sons of God, in anticipation of the promised Kingdom.

Confronted with the stark reality of our suffering people and with the all too indifferent sort of Christianity which distracts us from this reality with its promise of other-worldly happiness and its metaphysical speculations, the temptation to abandon the faith has been great. The temptation has been increased in intensity through contact with groups greatly influenced by MLMTT – the revolutionary theory which offers the analytical tools so necessary for the transformation of our society and the liberation of our people. Yet what has happened in the concrete? Our participation in the liberation struggle has given us a new self-awareness, a new consciousness which in the process has been reshaping us as Christians and has shown us new directions for renewal in faith and for purification of our Christianity.

The following is an attempt at formulating a new understanding of the Christian religion as seen in the light of the present Philippine situation analyzed from the perspective of MLMTT.

A. THE QUESTION OF FAITH

Proposition 1. Faith is subject to class analysis. Faith as lived in the concrete assumes 'class content'.

We are Christians with petty bourgeois origins trying to remould our petty bourgeois faith. The petty bourgeois character of faith reveals itself most clearly in the exuberant concern of the Christian for his own personal salvation and eternal happiness. The relationship of faith is considered a very private affair in which the Christian establishes a vertical relationship with God, wanting to be alone with him in blissful contact. The social dimension of this bourgeois faith is understood primarily in terms of almsgiving, 'loving God in the neighbour', etc., which serves to increase the personal merit of the Christian, rendering him worthy of union with God in heaven. In short, everything relates to the Christian's individualistic desire for eternal life. Such an orientation is reflective of the nature of the bourgeois class.

It is precisely in the struggle that such faith loses its meaning. If we are to re-orient it, we must look deeply into our class roots and class interests, which somehow give shape to this type of faith. If our faith is not freed from its false, bourgeois, mystical content, it can never hope to take the aspirations of our people seriously and thus can never stand up to the accusation of irrelevance.

Proposition 2. Faith must take on a revolutionary character by assuming the standpoint of the revolutionary classes, specifically, the proletarian standpoint.

Faith is commitment to Christ in our neighbour. The 'neighbour' should be no other than the oppressed masses in our society. Faith has to be partisan. It has to take the side of the poor and powerless in much the same way that Christ incarnated himself as a poor and powerless man. Faith has to include in its thrust the resolute commitment to love and serve the oppressed people; it has to be a total surrender to Christ in the love and service of the exploited and the oppressed.

In contrast to this proletarian standpoint of faith is the petty bourgeois standpoint of faith – the middle way that is for both the oppressed and the oppressor. Is this not the standpoint of those who say that faith is love of all men, all classes, and that the Church is supposed to serve all men, all classes? We believe that this petty bourgeois standpoint obscures the irreconcilable conflict between the antagonistic classes.

If faith is a conversion to Christ, it is also a conversion to our people. Such conversion can never take place unless we remould ourselves constantly and painstakingly by changing our outlook, divesting it of its bourgeois shape. Only then can we make the interests of our people our very own and see the proper social dimension of our faith.

Proposition 3. Faith in its evangelical content betrays its poverty in the task of restructuring society, and stands in need of scientific tools provided by a revolutionary theory such as MLMTT.

If faith's thrust is to be on the side of the oppressed people of our society, if it is to be of real service to this social sector, faith has to realize its own poverty in transforming the oppressive reality in our society through revolution. Faith, therefore, has to assume a dialogue with and necessarily integrate into itself the analysis of Philippine society, an analysis performed best by MLMTT. What results from this is a purification of faith. It is cleansed of its links with selfish class interests. It is understood more clearly as obedience to the call of liberation and as courage to take risks in the service of the revolution even to the point of death.

B. The Renewal of Theology

Proposition 1. Theology must be in the service of the struggle.

The fundamental question we raise is this: for whom is theology? A theology that is divorced from the concrete experience of our people in their struggle for liberation cannot be called their own. What we need today in the Philippines is a reflection on the faith experience of the people in their cry for justice, equality, and national democracy. We should be cautious of a theology that domesticates their longings and mystifies their experience of oppression into fatalism and resignation. At best, we must develop a theology in the interest and realization of their national and democratic aspirations.

In the face of today's fascist regime in the Philippines, some churchmen are popularizing a kind of a 'theology of collaboration', or a 'theology of critical cooperation', or a 'theology of resignation', which either directly supports or foolishly compromises with the dictatorial government. A theology that does not stimulate Christians to commit themselves to the liberation of the exploited and oppressed has nothing to say to them. Theologizing is futile toil if it does not contribute to the radical social change of peoples and institutions in our semi-feudal and semi-colonial society.

Specifically, we see that the task of theology today in the Philippines is to be a weapon in the cultural revolution. Theology is to be used (1) to criticize and destroy the feudal, bourgeois, and elitist Christianity the ruling classes are propagating in order to reinforce the unjust structures of a semi-feudal and semi-colonial society (in particular, we direct this weapon at the many attempts to use the name of the Lord and the Christian faith to lull our people into hopelessness and helplessness in the face of oppression); (2) to help mobilize Christians and non-Christians in the building of a new culture that will be nationalist, democratic, and scientific. We aim to use our theology in organizing and unifying our people so that they will liberate themselves and make their history as free sons of God.

Proposition 2.   Theology is subject to class analysis.

Mass versus elitist theology. At present, theologizing is an activity performed by a select group of professional theologians who wield considerable influence on church circles. By and large, these theologians have little or no contact with the experience of the broad masses of our people in the revolutionary struggle. More often than not, they depend on imported theological reflections from the Western world and feed these without much ado to the Filipino Christian. Their theology thereby reflects the mentality of the petty bourgeois Westernized class in Philippine society.

We believe that theological reflection should increasingly be a mass undertaking of the people of God in the Philippines. Professional theologians should consider themselves mere representatives and servants of the masses in their theological endeavour. In a manner of speaking, the Christian masses should be armed with the theological means of production and be educated to use these properly to reflect on their struggle towards liberation. In this way, professional theologians will no longer hold sway over the Christian masses.

Indigenized (Filipino) versus colonial theology. We could say that until now we are suffering from a kind of 'theological imperialism' of Western theologians on whom much, if not all, of our theological reflection depends. We cannot deny, however, that there has been a bit of reshaping or rehashing done by the local theologians especially in the seventies. Yet we are still quite remote from possessing a thoroughly indigenized theology that would take as its material basis the faith experience of the Filipino people in the context of the liberation struggle.

Proposition 3.   The reality of Philippine revolution must be a *locus theologicus* of Filipino theology. Theology has to situate itself in the context of the revolutionary struggle and thereby attain to a new understanding of the constants (dogmas) of faith and revelation, in the service of the people of God in the Philippines.

We need today, as Christians who are participating in the liberation struggle of our people, a theological thematization of Philippine revolution seen from the perspective of both the gospel and MLMTT. In the eyes of the Christian, the national democratic movement is not a purely secular movement, however much it is influenced by a secular ideology such as MLMTT. We feel that the activity of the Holy Spirit is a real force in the movement. If this is so, the same Spirit must want to say something to us Christians through the phenomenon of the revolutionary struggle. What does he want of the Church today in the face of the revolution? What does he demand from the communities of men in general? Theologically speaking, how do we assess the new forms of pastoral ministry being developed by priests in the underground? How do we view the 'a-political' Christian movements towards community building? What are the theological implications of the armed struggle of the oppressed class (90 per cent of whom are Christians) against their enemies in our society?

If the revolutionary struggle is central to the Filipino national experience, then theology has to situate itself in the context of such a struggle. Once situated thus, theology will truly succeed in reinterpreting and making relevant the constants (dogmas) of the faith and in the process put a genuine Filipino stamp on their meaning. Only then perhaps could we say that the Christian message has been truly incarnated in and thereby has liberated the Filipino soul.

C. THE NEW ROLE OF THE CHURCH

Proposition 1. The Philippine Church is subject to class analysis. It has class interests that are predominantly bourgeois. Historically, it has been identified with the ruling classes, and has by and large supported the *status quo*, particularly in its posture of neutrality and compromise.

The basic question to ask the Philippine Church concerns its class standpoint: whom is it for? If the Church is partisan, taking the side of the poor and the oppressed, then its historical role in the struggle becomes unmistakably clear. If it is to be of true service to the exploited people of our country, it should take an active part in the task of national and social liberation, employing the means at its disposal to fight for justice, truth and love. It has to be an agent of change, fostering most especially a revolutionary counter-culture, and contributing in its own particular way to the establishment of counter-institutions for the radical transformation of our society.

But if the Church would actively participate in the social transformation, it has to be no less scientific in carrying out its role. In
the past, our Church has been utterly a-historical and unscientific
in its approach to social problems. Yet, of course, the Church has
always pretended to be the defender of the poor. Its defence of the
poor, however, has been unmethodical, reformist and piecemeal. It
has never been able to pinpoint with precision who are *the* people
on whose side it has to be and who are their class enemies against
whom it has to take a definite stand, neither neutral nor com-
promising.

Unequipped with a revolutionary theory, the Church will forever
remain hampered in grasping the total picture of Philippine society,
which is characterized by social inequalities and plagued by social
demons of feudalism and imperialism. It will never be able to
correctly determine the principal and secondary contradictions
existing in Philippine society. Thus, it will have to content itself with
offering nothing more than palliatives and lifting a finger in fear and
hesitation to help the oppressed of the land without going deeper
into the roots of the problem.

Now is the time for the Church to go beyond merely raising its
prophetic voice against social injustice. Now is the time for it to dirty
its hands in active participation in the militant preparation of the
people of God in their struggle for a more just society. In the present
historical context, it has the responsibility of giving living witness
against the dictatorial regime of the present administration which
tramples upon the dignity and freedom of the people of God in this
country. Irresponsibility on its part in this regard can only be at the
cost of the people it seeks to serve.

Proposition 2. Church renewal through participation in the
struggle is imperative if we are to be true to our people and the
demands of the gospel.

While recognizing the fact that the Church as a whole may yet be
unprepared to take the radical line of such activist Christian groups
as the Christians for National Liberation (CNL), the Church
Renewal Movement (CRM), and the Kilusang Kristiyano ng
Kabataang Pilipino (KKKP), all underground organizations, we
make the following recommendations with regard to Church renewal
in the context of the revolutionary struggle.

(*a*) Democratization, or more accurately, democratic central-
ization of ecclesiastical institutions in order to give Christians in the
grass roots a more participatory role in the mission of the Church,

and to attain to greater efficiency in the implementation of consensus decisions. (This could be a witness against the one-man rule of the US-Marcos dictatorship in the country.)

(*b*) Radical renewal of liturgical worship in order that the more progressive elements of the faith could be brought into sharper focus in community celebrations, and the domesticating, mystifying interpretations of the gospel message – interpretations made under the influence of our corrupt, elitist, idealist, and colonial culture – could be superseded in the people's life of worship. Perhaps only then could the liturgy be expressive of the genuine aspirations of our people in the search for national democracy. Perhaps only then could we attain a liturgy of liberation.

(*c*) Re-orientation and redirection of our apostolates in order that they could be the means by which the Church could realize its role in the revolutionary struggle of our people.

(*d*) Re-orientation of seminary and religious training so that future Church leaders may be formed in the consciousness of their responsibility to be present in the very process of the people's struggle towards liberation.

(*e*) Study in depth of the Philippines situation as scientifically analyzed by the revolutionary theory of MLMTT, not only in traditional ecclesiastical institutions of education but also 'wherever two or three are gathered in the Lord's name'.

CONCLUSION

It would be all too ambitious of us to claim dogmatic clarity on all the points we have tried to reflect on regarding our experience as Christians actively involved in the liberation struggle of our people. What we have done is merely to ponder initially upon how our participation in the struggle under the influence of the revolutionary theory of MLMTT has affected us in our understanding of our faith, of theology, and the Church.

We have not touched on the global aspects of Christianity but dwelt merely on what seemed most essential at the present stage of our involvement. Principally, our reflections mirror a criticism, at times rather severe, of the Christian religion as we find it today in our country. Nothing has been mentioned about the positive aspects which have been taking shape at least in some segments of the Church since Vatican II. This is perhaps due to the fact that we are preoccupied with the urgency of reforms still to be carried out in attitudes, institutions, and outlooks in Philippine Christianity, if it is to be true to its ideals as a living religion in this country. We must confess that we are a bit impatient.

The urgency of transforming the type of Christianity being lived by the Filipino in the light of our experience as Christian activists has been more clearly recognized since we grasped the total Philippine situation through the scientific analysis of MLMTT. Here again, we have to admit the limits of our discussions, inasmuch as we did not attempt to define the limitations of MLMTT, but simply accepted the fact that it is very much alive and is being tested historically in practice in our country and not without valuable results. One of us, for instance, mentioned that his contact with MLMTT has given him both anger and hope concerning our people's plight: anger at the class enemies of the people trying to perpetuate the *status quo*, hope for the masses who will certainly achieve victory through the revolution. For all its biases, we are not quick to condemn MLMTT as 'dangerous' to the faith.

Perhaps the greatest contribution that MLMTT has given us is that it has sharpened our realization that the call of the hour is nothing less than the gift of ourselves in the service of our people in their struggle against their class enemies. We, as Christians, now understand more clearly that the 'neighbour' Christ talks about in the gospel is the people who want to liberate themselves from all forces that enslave them. Everything else is now secondary, even in the question of life itself. For our people must come first and foremost in our lives.

Yong-Bock Kim · *Koinonia and Struggle in Korea*

Yong-Bock Kim, 'Christian Koinonia in the Struggle and Aspirations of the People of Korea', *Asia Focus*, No. 661/1/77, pp.44–48

One of the characteristics of the Korean minjung democratic movement is Christian participation in the struggle. Now we turn specifically to the nature of the involvement of Korean Christians: a search for the historical vocation of Christians in Korea. At the present stage this historical vocation has emerged concretely in the form of a koinonia [fellowship] which has inserted itself into the midst of the historical contradictions of the people (minjung) in Korea.

It was in the 1973 Easter Sunrise Service that a small voice,

'Resurrection of democracy is the liberation of the people (minjung)' cried out. It was small, but not empty. It had power in a symbolic manner, because it was the bearer of historical consciousness both in terms of its contradictions and of its propensity toward historical transformation.

It was from this koinonia that the Theological Declaration of 1973 emerged and set the terms of the movement that unfolded among the Korean Christians and that went far beyond the boundary of the Christian fold. It was a manifesto of koinonia in search for the people's movement. In short, this little koinonia became the catalytic spearhead for the present democratic movement of the Korean people.

This koinonia had some distinct characteristics. (1) It had *a sense of history in terms of the stories of the people's suffering*. Therefore, the koinonia had a concrete historical consciousness of the social contradictions of the Korean people, physically and perceptually. One feature of this consciousness is that the koinonia understood the contradictions in terms of power relations. (2) *The koinonia was the bearer of messianic symbols*, drawn from Christianity. The language of Jesus as the Messiah for the poor and oppressed was a system of symbols that provided powerful resources to move ahead in an attempt to overcome the historical contradictions of the Korean people. There was no question that their Messiah was for the poor. They were the first ones who realized the power of the religion of the oppressed in a positive sense. (3) *They attempted to mobilize the powers and resources of the people* to create and catalyze a people's movement. Although this aspect has yet to emerge fully, there is no question that the political goals of the people and strategic questions rose in the process of their participation in the struggle. (4) Their goal has not been narrow, such as to seize power, but has been comprehensively historical in that *they sought a broad historical transformation*, and they believed that in such a transformation process the poor shall be liberated and the oppressed will find fulfillment. In this sense the little group of people was the paradigmatic koinonia that generated the dynamics of the present democratic movement and set the terms of it.

The koinonia was neither a tightly knit group, nor was it monolithic. It was an open community. For example, a koinonia has emerged in the Catholic church around JOC (Catholic Young Workers Organization) just as such a community has emerged around UIM (Protestant Urban Industrial Mission groups). Their styles of operation are slightly different, but the solidarity between them and their basic goals and intentionalities are one and the same. Today we witness a number of activities of such koinonia. There is the UIM koinonia, who insert themselves into the life of industrial, rural, and urban poor people. There are the Thursday prayer meetings of the families of political prisoners – a form of koinonia experience. There have emerged the meetings at Galilee Church of professors dismissed from their teaching posts due to their critical stance; another koinonia called Sarangbang Church has arisen among the poor urban 'squatters' out of their struggle against government slum clearance. The reality of koinonia is prominent among the wives and families of the 18 political prisoners who are under trial due to their Declaration of National Democratic Salvation (March 1, 1976). The Priests' Corps for the Realization of Democracy, Korean Student Christian Federation and related youth groups manifest clearly the reality of koinonia.

The inner experience of the koinonia has been that of suffering – a participation in the suffering of the people. This suffering is a most powerful experience on the symbolic level as well as on the physical and spiritual level for the Christian community and for the people of Korea, because it is suffering that is being experienced innocently under political repression. The contradiction between the innocent suffering and the justice of God forms the matrix of the historical process seen theologically, which opens the door for the transformative process. It is here that the Cross as the Christian symbol of suffering, and Resurrection as the symbol of new koinonia become real. Therefore suffering entails new self and new koinonia. It is in the context of this suffering that koinonia undergoes the process of self-transformation.

The history of suffering is that of the people caught in historical contradictions; and yet suffering does not necessarily make a new people without the process of transformation, which is paradigmatically initiated, often by messianic koinonia or its equivalent. This tradition of suffering of the messianic koinonia started with the martyrdom of the Catholic koinonia during the later part of the Yi dynasty, under the political suppression of the Yangban rulers. The word 'suffering' gained a new meaning in Korean culture and history through the martyrdom of the Catholic koinonia, which was inserted into the social contradictions of the Yi society, especially the contradictions rising our of class relations between the Yangban rulers and the common people. The suffering community of Catholics began to identify with the suffering of the people, and the community as the bearer of the messianic and utopian symbols triggered the beginning of a process of historical transformation. Yet at this point in history of the Korean people, the Catholic koinonia remained more a potential than an actual transformative force.

The indigenous transformative koinonia, the Tonghak movement, rose in the 1860's, and gave birth to the Tonghak political movement, from the Tonghak Rebellion to the March First Independence Movement, in an attempt to overcome both internal and external contradictions in the history of the Korean people at the end of the 19th century and the beginning of the 20th century. The Tonghak religious koinonia as the bearer of the messianic and utopian symbol system gave impetus to the Tonghak peasant movement to overcome the social contradictions of the late Yi society; after the Japanese annexation of Korea the Tonghak koinonia also became the backbone of the March First Independence Movement of the Korean people.

On the other hand the Christian Protestant community was formed in the late 19th century. From the beginning it took root in the bottom echelon of Korean society and was immediately immersed in the historical contradictions of Korean society and its people. The Protestant community as the bearer of a messianic symbol system triggered a social transformation process, dealing with social customs on a minute level and with political questions on a large scale. When the koinonia that bears messianic or utopian symbols enters into the depths of historical contradictions, it creates a dynamics of movement of the people for historical transformation. Thus, Protestant koinonia and Tonghak koinonia when they were inserted into the contradictions, generated powerful movements of the people to overcome the contradictions through structural transformation in internal and external power relations.

The Christian community, Protestant and Catholic, particularly small koinonia, have entered into the center of the contradictions of Korean society today. These social contradictions had to do with the structures of economic and social injustices in the life of the people in the factories, in the urban squatter areas, and in rural areas. These koinonia were thrust into the area of political contradictions, which were expressed structurally as the military dictatorship of the Yushin Revitalization system.

This koinonia, in short, as the bearer of the messianic symbol system, enters into the center of historical contradictions, be they on the economic, political, social, or cultural levels; then it releases a powerful dynamic of historical transformation toward a new integration of historical process. In this process a people's movement rises to change the structure of history and in this context, new language and new ideology, new humanity and new society emerge in history. The Korean situation is in the throes of such historical transformation today in the midst of democratic struggle.

The consciousness of Christian koinonia described above is not religious, but *historical*. It is not based upon dogmatic theology of the Church or systematic theology of Christendom. It is a sense of historical vocation and historical praxis in the midst of the people's (minjung) struggle for liberation. Therefore, the liberating reflection of koinonia can only take place (1) when *it is radically liberated from the religious, cultural, intellectual and institutional*, structures of Western Christendom and its 'colonies' in which we live as captives to a large extent, and (2) when the *Koinonia inserts itself into the historical contradictions*, opening us to the suffering people, and *listens to the messianic invitation of Jesus Messiah to the suffering people for the messianic feast.*

Professor Moon of Hankuk Theological Seminary boldly proposes a radical break from the Western theological systems, and calls for authentic theological reflection which rises out of the midst of the people's struggle, and he also calls for a dialogue with Black Theologies of Liberation and Latin American Theologies of Liberation, not to imitate, but to learn from and share with them. At the same time, Prof. Moon also calls upon the koinonia to learn from the oppressed Minjung in order to have authentic historical consciousness. He writes,

The Korean Church still regards as their own, theologies which were manufactured in the Western churches. Moreover, each denomination establishes its own theological seminaries and teaches its (Western) theological traditions. This situation must be overcome as soon as possible. With all our intellect and might we must do our best in the search for authentic theology, reading the Bible. Then there will emerge our authentic theology that will liberate us in Korea and that will contribute to the peoples of the world for a new tomorrow.

Prof. Suh of Yonsei University advances a similar theme in theological manner.

The revolutionary power of the Gospel has remained suppressed under the oppression of religious institutions of the Christian religion. The eschatological message of revolution for the coming new age was contained by Christendom; and the promise of the Gospel was reflected into the other world, which has no relation with the historical future ... Now in the post-Christian world, where the Church is dissolved, the gospel manifests its revolutionary power, and becomes the religion of the poor, oppressed, Amhareth and Minjung. This is the new historical horizon.

The koinonia takes up its vocation in the radically historical situation outside of church history in the post-Christian world. This is especially an imperative for Asian Christians, for they are only a small segment of Asian peoples. Therefore, the consciousness of the koinonia does not rise from the Christian Church's pure religious experiences, but it becomes clear as historical consciousness when it inserts itself into the historical contradictions and participates in the people's struggle. This means that the historical consciousness of the koinonia finds its historical reference in the story of the people: the suffering and aspiration of the people. The Theological Declaration of Korean Christians of 1973 states the relationship between the people and koinonia:

The people in Korea are looking up to Christians and urging us to take action in the present grim situation. It is not because we deserve to represent them. We have often fallen short of their deeper expectations, and yet we are urged and encouraged to move on this course of action, because we are moved by their agony to call upon God for their deliverance from evil days.

Then, what is unique about the historical consciousness of Christian koinonia? The Christian koinonia is determined by messianic consciousness in the process of historical transformation in which the suffering of the people is resolved and their aspirations are continually realized towards liberation. The primary paradigm of the messianic koinonia is found in the history of the people of Israel: the Koinonia of Jesus which was inserted into the contradictions of the people of Israel. In this process the Christian movement of the oppressed people for liberation emerged in the first centuries of Christian history. Thus, the story of the people of Israel has a parabolic significance for the story of the peoples of the world; and Jesus' koinonia has paradigmatic significance for the Christian koinonia in the history of the oppressed peoples throughout the world. Therefore, the task of historical reflection of the Christian koinonia is to release the power of the messianic message into the process of historical transformation in which the people struggle to overcome their suffering and to realize their hopes. In this process the messianic message is embodied in historical language, and its messianic vision is historicalized. Therefore, not only must we liberate the reading of the Bible from hermeneutical and dogmatic straitjackets on the one hand, but we should also guard against illusory and a-historical reading of it. The story of the Bible as the story of the people of Israel should be exposed *immediately* to the story of the people in Asia, so that the power of the Gospel may effect a liberation process by the immediate mediation of the koinonia's witness in the midst of the people's struggle.

We have distinguished here koinonia and established Church and their respective consciousness. Theology has been of the Church, not of history. This is particularly true of Western Christendom. The Church's dogmatic position and theological outlook has usually been determined by its cultural environment and social class, whereas the koinonia is relatively free of cultural and social determinations, and the messianic symbols and messianic consciousness which koinonia bears release transformative power, when inserted into the historical contradictions.

We also must distinguish the koinonia from the political party or other power groupings. Koinonia can never substitute for the party. The koinonia as the bearer of the messianic language catalyzes the people's movement which transforms history, revolutionizes power relations, economic and political, radically alters social institutions, and creates the new values of the people. And yet the koinonia and party must be distinguished though they are both integral parts of the people's revolutionary process. One should not be reduced to the other; they must maintain distinct identity and function in creative interaction with each other. This means that the messianic consciousness, though it should be embodied in ideological and other historical realities, cannot be reduced simply to the ideological or cultural. The messianic consciousness of the koinonia should constantly remain as the transcendent or even transient dynamic to the new future, as it is constantly and continually inserting itself into historical contradictions as they become clear.

Josef Widyatmadja · *Incarnation as Subversion*

Josef Widyatmadja, 'Towards a Theology of People', document published by the Christian Conference of Asia, 1977, pp.92–93,95–99

The way to achieve peace and liberation is not easy. The cost to be paid is very expensive. Total commitment is needed for every one who fights for justice, freedom and man's hope. Without love it is impossible for man to fight for justice and freedom for his fellow man. To stand and take side with his people, Moses had to leave Pharaoh's palace and become fugitive. He had to wander for forty years together with his father-in-law. It was not possible for Moses to stand as an Egyptian authority, who fought for his people's destiny. Moses experienced what it meant when Pharaoh recognized him as an Israelite. He had to stand and be in a row with suffering people. Pharaoh's wealth and inheritance did not make Moses indifferent or cause him to hesitate taking risk in liberating his people from slavery.

The whole ministry of Jesus Christ was a subversive action. No doubt that incarnation created commotion, restlessness and even brought victims, hundreds of babies slain in Bethlehem. Incarnation caused Joseph and Maria to become fugitives and flee to Egypt. Every attempt of transformation for peace, freedom and hope creates commotion and subversive accusation. Transformation is not possible without opposition.

The sermons of Jesus contained new and radical facts. His Sermon on the Mount shook the existing teachings. His presence among the tax collectors and His friendship with a prostitute caused anger to the Pharisees. He was regarded as disgracing His holiness as a prophet. His cure of a blind man and a cripple on the Sabbath was considered as breaking the Law. Jesus' preaching in the temple gave a character of His ministry to liberate man from oppression and misery.

The existence of the Kingdom of God in the midst of the world was assumed by Jesus as yeast to leaven bread. Its influence is slow, invisible, but carrying out a total change in its surroundings. Jesus never maintained the status quo. His ministry never used harshness and was never demonstrative. He often forbade His disciples to glorify Him. He forbade the man who was cured to tell about Him. He often withdrew from the crowd that was looking for Him.

The whole life and ministry of Jesus never got rid of the supervision of the religious authority of his time. He was always spied on by the Pharisees and the scribes. His enemies always attempted to find faults in His sayings and teachings. He was often ridiculed by questions. The Korean Christians, as well as the Korean people, their actions and their expressions are not free from KCIA's supervision. Terror is done by KCIA. Those who are arrested by KCIA are not communist agents or those who possess a liberation army for a revolution, but those who have a commitment to suffering people, because democracy and human values are trampled in Korea. Kim Chi Ha is a Catholic poet. Meetings and religious services in Korea are not free from KCIA's supervision. Interrogations of Koreans in Japan are also held by KCIA. The meaning of incarnation and Christ's suffering in Asia is more obvious in the midst of suffering and oppression experienced by the Korean people, and also by the Philippine people. Asian churches in the midst of development and industrialization need a sense of understanding about Jesus Christ's incarnation. In following the pace of development in Asia, the pioneers of development are not standing any more as a union serving the people and community, but they have to transform themselves among the people. The role as prophet and priest in the Old Testament did not result in redemption and total peace. Only through incarnation can there be redemption and total peace. Without incarnating himself amidst the people, it is impossible to understand the suffering and hope of the people. The pompous planning, carried out by the technocrats in development offices, deviated very much from the basic needs of the people. The meaning of hunger, feeling cold, being captured and having one's house torn down will not possibly be understood by political leaders, technocrats and businessmen. It is impossible that those persons will fight for the interest of the people, because they have never lived and suffered together with the people. They never know the hope of the suffering people. Incarnation among the suffering people will lead to an understanding of the real hope of the people.

The purpose of incarnation is transformation and alteration. Every transformation certainly causes opposition and conflict. The birth of Jesus in the world caused opposition from King Herod and the scribes. Conflict cannot be avoided by the incarnation of the Son of God. Without conflict there are not transformation, redemption, peace and mercy possible.

The whole ministry of Jesus was full of conflict. He never obeyed the law unreservedly. He did not change the law but fulfilled it. Jesus' view about the law was not the same as the scribes' or the

Roman government's (Herod and Pontius Pilate). Jesus was not under the obedience of human law, but He stood in an absolute obedience to His Father God. His prayers in Gethsemane reflected Jesus' obedience to His Father.

The problems of development and liberation in Asia can not be separated from the possibility of conflict against the existing authority. Every change toward a 'welfare' society (kingdom of shalom) often gets challenges from the established party. Here the churches in Asia cannot take a neutral attitude. They have to take side with those who are weak and tortured by the unjust structure or they will maintain and strengthen the position of the oppressors.

There are two kinds of conflict: open violence and disguise without visible confrontations. Neither kind of conflict is possible today in Asia. Yet the potential for conflict cannot be ignored. Priests, community organizers and Asian people in general often find themselves in a dilemma between siding with the people and being considered lawbreakers by the government, or siding with the authorities but ignoring the law of love and human dignity. Where shall we stand?

Every struggle will pass through suffering, but where there is struggle, there is hope. Hope is something we don't reach yet. Paul said: '. . . But hope that is seen is not hope; for what a man seeth, why doth he yet hope for?' (Romans 8:24)

There is no resurrection without the cross and death of Jesus Christ. For if we have been planted together in the likeness of his death, we shall be also in the likeness of his resurrection. (Romans 6:5) Stephen, Peter, John and the martyrs held firm in the teaching and confession of Jesus who had already resurrected. Suffering, torture and accusation of subversion did not disturb their will to defend the sick and the weak. Acts 4:9 says: 'If we this day be examined of the good deed done to the impotent man, by what means he is made well.' Many incidents have struck the members of the urban industrial mission in Asia because of its testimony and ministry to those who are weak, sick and tortured. The organizers fighting in the midst of the relocated or dislocated communities, oppressed workers and farmers exploited by landlords have been declared subversive by the authorities. They were captured, brought before the court and tortured. Torture can not discourage their resistance, because in spite of all the sufferings and tortures they have undergone, they live on the hope of a new world.

Those who are detained due to the charge of subversion need not be ashamed, because they know and realize the meaning of freedom and human rights to human life. The suffering they have endured did not equal the hope they obtained in the resurrection of Jesus. Paul in his epistle to the Philippians, said: 'According to my earnest expectation and my hope, that in nothing I shall be ashamed, but that with all boldness, as always, so now also Christ shall be magnified in my body, whether it be by life or by death. For me to live is Christ, and to die is gain. But if I live in the flesh, this is the fruit of my labor, yet what I shall choose I know not. (Philippians 1:20–22) Now the members of the Urban Industrial Mission are at a crossroad. Whether to live yielding independence, justice, people's power or to die in prison? Death does not frighten them to withdraw and betray the people who live in slavery.

Do the members of the Urban Industrial Mission have to be disappointed when they fail to organize people, are captured and their projects closed down? In attempting to fight for justice in the midst of the Asian people, failure and prison are not our standard. When the disciples of Lord Jesus were proud of the result of their work, because they had been able to cast out demons, to tread on scorpions, etc. Jesus gave them a warning: 'Notwithstanding, in this rejoice not that the spirits are subject unto you; but rather rejoice because your names are written in heaven.' (Luke 10:20) If the members of the Urban Industrial Mission emphasized their victory, their success in their struggle amidst Asian people, then in a short time the Urban Industrial Mission movement would disappear from the Asian soil. The measure of our joy in this ministry lies in the spirit which never dies in the people's struggle in Asia, not in the success or victory. The spirit of never giving up, loyal to the struggle until the end of life, is a standard of success of the Urban Industrial Mission. There was no resurrection and victory of Jesus without passing through crucifixion and failure. Broken spirit, retreating halfway, leaving the Asian people's struggle are failures in our mission. The success of the Asian people's struggle and of the members of UIM lies in the spirit and hope, which are never extinguished amidst the suffering of the Asian people.

The meaning of 'people' in New Testament is not similar to the meaning of *ethnos* or union based on skin's colour and language. People is also not similar to the meaning of *ochlos* or multitudes (gathering people). Both the meanings of *ethnos* and *ochlos* cannot be applied to the meaning of people. *Ethnos* is a more closed union based on skin's colour and language, whereas *ochlos* is a mass-gathering without any direction and certain commitment. It is a gathering of unorganized people, has no political awareness, etc.

Churches may develop into a unified *ethnos*, an alliance that has a racial nature and is very closed. The existing alliance is very closed. Its dogma and teachings become a criterion for participation, replacing the alliance based on skin colour or language.

Churches may also develop into an *ochlos*, an open union without any firm foundation, direction and a clear destination. No commitment to support a total liberation message. Each thinks and acts for his own interest without considering or supporting mutual tasks in the world. Another man's suffering is not a criterion for meeting one another in a place called a place of worship. The liberation message of Jesus Christ does not form any encouragement to organize an alliance; each fights for his own safety.

Churches must not fall into either that meaning of *ethnos* or *ochlos*. The church is people chosen by God to bring about the liberation message ... a *laos*/people. This new alliance is open for all people who have commitment toward the liberating message. This alliance has a clear direction and destination, namely to realize the signs of the kingdom of God in the midst of the world. This alliance is called to carry out social change, a change toward justice. This alliance will not take side with the oppressor, but it will be together with those who are oppressed. And the price which must be paid by this alliance is risk, cross and death.

The church in the midst of the world has three vocations, namely as 'king', 'priest' and 'prophet'. As 'priest', the church will pray for the government and the people. As 'king', church plays the role as defender of the poor and oppressed. It will stand to defend those who are treated unjustly, not to say amen and to support the oppressing authority. As 'prophet', it will warn the kings and authorities, who do injustice to their people.

If church means *ethnos*, then its obedience to the government is absolute. My government right or wrong. If church means *ochlos*, then it has no standpoint. It will be moved only by its own interest. For the sake of its own existence, the church often supports wrong actions by the government viz. unjust actions.

The obedience of the people of God is a critical obedience. Their obedience to God is absolute, whereas their obedience to their government has a limited nature. The people of God will only obey a government, as long as it does not abuse the authority received from God only to enrich itself, to oppress people and to sell its country to foreigners. Do the churches as people of God have to obey a government, which oppresses human rights and freedom and becomes greedy for wealth? There are many examples in the Old

Testament reflecting the attitudes of the prophets toward authoritarian government.

The commitment of the people of God, especially toward people's suffering and hope, often collides with the interest of the authorities. When social workers or community developers are confronted with the interest and hope of the people, they often incline to parallel their ministry with the interest of the government. They want to be neutral between two opposite hopes, between government and people, between workers and employers, between farmers and land-tenants.

Many rural development programs have only the projects for greening the land, giving fertiliser, giving help for irrigation and animal husbandry, but never touch or analyse the unjust system of marketing or the exploitation of farmers by landlords. Many irrigation and greening programs strengthen only the status quo, giving more profits to the landlords. The agricultural production in a village may increase, but it does not increase the welfare of the poor farmers; they are permanently robbed of their just share.

The development programs carried out by the churches in Asia should lead to transforming the unjust system, putting more pressure on those who are responsible for taking decisions, increasing the role of the people to take part in making decisions. Otherwise it would be better for the churches in Asia to stop their programs, because they will only aggravate the people's suffering and kill the people's hope.

8 · Ecology and Community

During the last two centuries many elements of Christian faith have been taken up in an increasingly secular culture, from the utopian striving for the kingdom of man to the more recent preoccupation with inner space. Other elements have proved less attractive to the modern age, notably the Fall. The Bible opens with a panoramic view of the potential of man and the world. It is not a primordial state but if anything an eschatological vision. For between the present and that final condition there is the reality of enmity between man and nature. Psychology has shown an interest in the alienation of man from God, political theory has been concerned with the alienation of man from man (or woman). But what are we to make of the myth of alienation from nature? Yet it is a recurring theme. In a messianic hymn the psalmist envisages a new harmony. 'The wolf shall dwell with the lamb, and the leopard shall lie down with the kid, and the calf and the lion and the fatling together, and a little child shall lead them.' The condition of such harmony is the appearance of the man of righteousness. It may even be that this connection is behind the passing reference in the Temptation, 'and he was with wild beasts. . . .' But it is given more definitive expression in the claim of Paul. 'For the creation waits with eager longing for the revealing of the sons of God . . .'

A stirring claim, but myth raised upon myth, the second Adam overcoming the effects of the first. What are we to make of it? Eschatology lends itself to extravagance and refuses the constraints of empirical tests. But how can such extravagances be explained – or explained away – to the sophisticated age, the cultured who dismiss if they cannot be passionate enough to despise? Yet strange to recount, this claim from the Bible, this recurring theme of domination-and-alienation, of righteousness-and-harmony, has in our own day taken on both the urgency of eschatology and the realism of bread. Like the ancient prophets of the Day of the Lord, the 'futurists' as they are called, thunder against the excesses of the day, against the injustices of a divided (world) society, against those who live for the present without a thought of what must surely follow, against those who think that in spite of all warnings disaster will never overtake them.

Without the prompting of religion, ecologists have made clear an ancient riddle. Man can have dominion over the earth and make it like a garden. But it must be the righteous man who deals fairly. The man of domination alienates nature and distorts it with his own fallen will. The ancient riddle is not to be dismissed or hidden in embarrassment from the modern age. Rather it has been powerfully confirmed.

If anything the positions have been reversed. The old mythology has been confirmed, while the new mythology of growth has been exposed as the most dangerous false consciousness. The crisis confronts us but Western capitalism is prepared to take a desperate gamble. The Bible claims that harmony comes only with the righteous man: capitalism gambles on the contrary view, that righteousness is a luxury which we cannot afford at the moment. After we have got the economy right, then perhaps . . . But for the moment principles would betray us. So Lord Keynes predicted some forty years ago. 'But beware. The time for all this is not yet. For at least another hundred years we must pretend to ourselves and to everyone that fair is foul and foul is fair; for foul is useful and fair is not. Avarice and usury and precaution must be our gods for a little longer still. For only they can lead us out of the tunnel of economic necessity into daylight.'

Nor is such unprincipled materialism peculiar to capitalism. What vision did Khruschev set before the Russian people as he led them Moses-like from Stalinist bondage? His exhortation was 'Catch up and surpass the United States.' His grand plan was that the Soviet Union would overtake the United States in significant areas by 1970 and in all areas by 1980. In other words socialism would be vindicated as the more efficient way of arriving at the goals of capitalism.

But now even the house-prophets of growth are refusing to accept the myth any longer. From the Massachusetts Institute of Technology itself comes a warning of 'the limits of growth' while The Club of Rome is concerned with 'mankind at the turning point'. The experts are far from agreed. Predictions are no better than the material on which they are based. And so we have 'the computor that printed out wolf'. It has become fashionable to berate the futurists as prophets of doom. Such popular words of comfort also have precedent in biblical history and there has never been a lack of players in Emperor Nero's Fiddle Band.

When experts disagree on minor issues the rest of us might wait and see. But when the stakes involve the future of life on this planet we cannot risk leaving the debate in their hands. But the issue in any case is one which touches on fundamentally religious points. It has been said that if we listened to history it would not have to repeat itself. Do we honestly believe that we can achieve ends which are in complete contradiction to the means necessary to arrive at them: fair is foul and foul is fair? Do we honestly believe that we in the West can continue to live as we do, recruiting a kind of Magnificent Scientific Seven to fight our problems for us and deliver us from the ills which are endemic to our life-style? The problem is of our own making and it cannot be solved merely by a technological solution. For this reason E. F. Schumacher speaks of two reactions to the situation, those of 'the forward stampede' and those whom he calls 'home-comers'. The latter he sees in terms of the Beatitudes, that revolutionary manifesto which overturns all the pretentions of worldly wisdom.

The same theme appears in the work of Robert Stivers. 'Neither technical nor political solutions *alone* will suffice.' We are part of the problem and its solution. For this reason I have included in this chapter sections from David Clark's recent book on communities, sub-titled: 'Towards an Alternative Society'. Stivers is able to quote Lord Keynes also, this time on the changes required in the transition to the utopian future envisaged by the economist. 'I think with dread of the readjustment of habits and instincts of the ordinary man, bred into him for countless generations, which he may be asked to discard within a few decades.' But what, asks Stivers, if the adjustment should be not to a Keynesian future, but to a much more modest 'sustainable society'? How much more demanding the readjustments. To continue the biblical analogy, we may recall that such doubts plagued the prophets who required the people, 'Choose this day ...' How could they be asked to give up what they had? Yet one choice was, in Schumacher's sense, a 'home-coming'. Not superficially the more attractive choice, but one which brought them a step closer to that coincidence of righteousness-and-harmony.

David Clark introduces us to many different communities, most of which are in some way concerned with life-style. It is as well not to be romantic about communities – even religious communities. Perhaps we should say, especially religious communities. The book contains some salutary criticisms of the various types. Many of them are dependent on the continued existence of the very society they claim to reject. As Geoffrey Crowther claims, 'Forming a commune became another form of consumer fetishism.' Yet the formation of communities is a realistic response to a complex problem of which we are the primary ingredient. As yet it may be too early to require that they create an alternative society or an alternative reality, yet their existence, with all its associated problems, helps to undermine the credibility of the mythology within which most of us live. And if they sometimes seem odd by the standards of society at large, then they may be, in the sense of the words of Fritz Perls, 'losing their minds but coming to their senses'.

David Clark · *Towards an Alternative Society*

David Clark, *Basic Communities*, SPCK 1977, pp.91–92, 56–57, 27–28, 99–100 106–9

'Avoid the use of disposable diapers.... Learn to cook from scratch.... Cut down on shower time.... Stop smoking.... Use lunch boxes instead of paper bags. ...' Just a few exhortations from the fifty-eight in a leaflet issued by Dartmouth House in 1975 as part of their environmentalist campaign. The battle is on: against waste and pollution and for care and conservation. What but a few years ago was seen as something of the latest bandwagon has now become a matter of serious and articulate concern.

Three aspects of society's material well-being are particularly worrying. There is anxiety that the flow of energy and raw materials, until recently taken for granted, will slowly cease; there is the realization that industry and its products have within them the power fatally to upset the delicate balance of the biosphere; and there is the awareness that our technology as it is, let alone as it might become, could well do more to destroy than enhance man's welfare. The response to these concerns has been kaleidoscopic, ranging from the dissemination of many erudite or hortatory articles and books to a new zeal for self-sufficiency and the development of an alternative technology. Linked to this has been the search for a new life-style, personal and communal, which has placed a major emphasis on simplicity and moderation especially with regard to

consumer patterns, and on working within the boundaries set by
nature rather than wealth.

Within this movement, for it can by now be called that, the Christian has been prominent. E. F. Schumacher, author of *Small is
Beautiful*, makes no apology for his own Christian stance and the
Bishop of Winchester's *Enough is Enough* has proved a bestseller.
Therefore, in seeking to use as illustrative material for this chapter
ventures which are Christian in ethos or in which Christians are
known to be actively involved, I do not feel I am distorting the
overall picture or underrating the major contribution of the non-
Christian in this field. My aim is not to produce a treatise on
conservation programmes or alternative technology; it is to assess
how what is happening reflects or affects the nature of power and
authority on the one hand, and the personal and interpersonal
dimensions of life on the other. As Ralf Dahrendorf comments in his
1974 Reith Lectures: 'After all, survival is not enough, what matters
is life worth living.'

Can and dare communities, however, break the circle in the other
direction by at times deliberately moving out of their enclaves to
risk direct encounter with the wider world? Some, such as the Community of Celebration, Post Green, and Findhorn, do this by exercising an external ministry which is supposedly their *raison dêtre*,
though again one wonders whether it is the actual ministry or the
quality of the community expressing it which impresses more. Other
groups believe that they have no 'call' to do anything but their own
thing within their limited circle, and there is much to be said for
inconspicuous living. Family communes as ends in themselves
form the main theme of the recent thorough investigation of the
secular scene by Philip Abrams and Andrew McCulloch. Their
inquiry led them to conclude that a random scattering of self-
contained units is the best description of the modern commune
'movement' in Britain. From the point of view of this book, however,
and especially in relation to those communities associated with the
Christian outlook, it must be said that unless they can in some way
extend their boundaries, initially perhaps in the direction of other
communities, and show that they can live as happily with those
as unlike as like themselves, then not much of major social significance has occurred.

Such openness to wider contacts and relationships is a matter of
great consequence for the relevance of communities to our time.
To move from the potential restrictiveness of the nuclear family into

the wider circle of a community may be, though by no means certainly, an initial step towards exploring the possibilities of intimacy and love at a time when free association, for good or ill, is fast becoming common-place. Jessie Bernard has persuasively argued that the looser co-operative household or intentional community, if not the rather intense commune, has a real future. There is an immense fund of vitality, spontaneity, and sheer enjoyment within many such ventures. Despite all difficulties, one feels that people have discovered a new sense of personal worth and a new depth in interpersonal relationships. Yet to stop there can lead to the establishment of narcissistic groups which teach us little. Philip Abrams and Andrew McCulloch at the end of their inquiry into self-contained secular family communes in Britain suggest that the wisest policy is to leave such groups severely alone. But from where we stand, the value of communal living is not whether it provides happy huddles for hairy or holy ones. It is whether it can train people in the art of living and loving which is able to reach beyond the security of even extended units into the vulnerability of a hostile, lonely, and apathetic world and there demonstrate a new and revolutionary dimension of human relationships. In what follows I examine the ways in which some basic communities are seeking to do just that.

British communities are strongly middle-class in membership and ethos, whatever age-group one is talking about. Most participants have received a good education and come from relatively affluent backgrounds, even if they have deliberately turned their backs on such a style of life. There are, however, two exceptions.

At one end of the social scale a significant number of the wealthy upper class, including the aristocracy, are directly or indirectly involved in promoting ventures in communal living. For example, Post Green is the home of Sir Thomas and Lady Lees. Ammerdown House is situated on Lord Hylton's estate, and Lady Ursula Burton of Dochfour House near Inverness is keenly interested in encouraging young people in their search for new patterns of community life. The Open Centres in particular have a fairly wealthy and sophisticated group behind them.

At the other end of the social scale, Bugbrooke has a large working-class element, amongst whom are young people who have run into personal difficulties of one kind or another. Other communities exist which have been set up to care for those who are disadvantaged or homeless. For example, the Cyrenian houses and

Simon communities contain a mix of the destitute and middle-class 'workers', the Pilsdon staff share their lives with many seeking social rehabilitation, the community at Bystock Court provides for mothers in need of care, and the Kingsway Community contains ex-drug takers. More will be said in a later chapter about such communities dedicated to the work of caring. But there are no intentional communities known to me which have been initiated or are run predominantly by those whom one could call working-class (Bugbrooke, for example, possessing some highly educated and very articulate leaders), though some from this social class, notably skilled manual workers, are here and there carrying considerable responsibilities.

The intentional communities of which I am writing have made little contact with the black population of this country. This is not, I believe, because of any latent racial prejudice within the community movement but because as yet the West Indians, Africans, and Asians are too intent on preserving and strengthening their own cultural and religious identity, the 'colony phenomenon', as it has been called, to want to become involved with white ventures in community-making. Until the black or white person can move out of his own racial grouping without fear of ostracism from those he leaves or of suspicion from those he joins, I see the emergence of communities of a racially integrated kind as still a very long way off. Basic communities do not exist apart from society in the human problems they face.

George Ineson at Taena writes along similar lines:

> The primary elements of any attempt to change our direction are (1) to use only tools which we can control and not those which control us; (2) to reverse the present addiction to the new as a status symbol – to care for the things we use so that they will last as long as possible and to use as little as we can instead of as much; (3) to be more aware of the results of our actions on other people and on the natural world so that we can reduce the harm we do; (4) to remember and rediscover the creative relationship between man and the work he does on and to the natural world.

There are, however, problems associated with these kind of suggestions about our use of the world's resources. As with 'Life Style', the initial impact of which has rather faded, there is often lacking a core group which can sustain enthusiasm. It is the vitality of the basic community rather than the conservationist guidelines which give continuing impetus to self-discipline. Dartmouth House, the Ashram Community, and Taena have gained here, but even so their ideas for a personal conservationist code are at times so numerous and so all-embracing as to be overwhelming, in the sense that it would take the utmost, indeed almost obsessive, vigilance not to infringe the code regularly, as well as a great deal of time and even expense to be fully loyal to it.

One other difficulty is that few communities (be they specifically dedicated to ecological concerns or not) attempting to live out a simpler life-style, would have been unable to get off the ground at all, and in certain cases survive, without drawing on wealth acquired through working the capitalist system. Centres such as Post Green, Ammerdown, and several groups in the Inverness area, as the monasteries before them, have wealthy and generous patrons. Others such as the Community of Celebration and more recently Findhorn, are backed by funds from the United States. Numerous communities have members who have been able to make their move on the basis of capital acquired in a world they now wish to question in one way or another. Of the fragmenting secular Commune Movement, Geoff Crowther makes a more generally relevant comment:

> The Commune Movement became a predominantly middle-class oriented body since it was only people from this background who could collect the necessary assets, both in terms of money and education, to be in a position to even consider taking off for the country. In this way they highlighted their privileged position and many 'communes' became glorified weekend cottages. 'Forming a commune' became another form of consumer fetishism.

Crowther does not believe all such ventures worthless, but he does point out the inherent dualism of alternatives which to survive have to draw heavily on the resources of the society criticized. Some communities, such as Findhorn, can even become affluent, and their enterprise border on commercialization, as a result of their popularity and professional publicity. On the other hand a conference of the Network for Alternative Technology and Technology Assessment in 1976 generally accepted that to refuse all State aid or the support of patrons was naive and that the criterion was not the source of funds so much as the extent to which 'the project or campaign helps to shift the balance of power'. None the less, in whatever way set up and backed, no one can ignore the dedication and often considerable personal sacrifice of those determined to build some model of a society which does not exploit, pollute, or look upon the creation of more and more wealth as the God-given right of man.

It would be naive to imagine that any of the projects discussed above are *the* key to the future. There are many peculiarities about their situation which prevents easy translation to our economy as we know it at present.

A fundamental difficulty is that of seeking to establish any style of genuinely participatory socialism within or over against an economy which, whether a Conservative or a Labour government be in power, is dominated by the profit motive, the market, and consumerism. Only the benevolent, the wealthy patrons of certain communities, or the philanthropic like Ernest Bader, are prepared to step somewhat out of line. Even here, as Schumacher notes, the backlash is not far off with even Bader's 'quiet revolution' still unacceptable to many (management *and* unions) in industry.

There are many ways in which this unacceptability becomes obvious, not least in the attempt by such enterprises to raise capital, which Father McDyer at Glencolumbkille states as one of his outstanding problems; though Glencolumbkille is fortunate for it does have an abundance of land, a commodity which in England is less available than in nearly any other country in the world. (This fact, incidentally, is probably one of the main reasons for the relatively few intentional communities here, especially in the ecological field, compared, for example, with the United States.)

It is thus easy for cynics, let alone outright antagonists, to employ the adjective 'parasitical' of such ventures. Geoff Crowther writes about the Commune Movement:

> Great lip-service was paid to the concept of self-sufficiency, yet this disguised a strong element of bourgeois escapism. Almost without exception these self-sufficient groups continued to be reliant on piped water, grid electricity, gas, transport and the petrochemical industry, etc., etc., all of which presupposed the continued existence of the things they had wanted to get away from.

There is some truth here and a few groups live in a kind of fantasy world until the need for medical services or schooling becomes acute. The older children from remote Scoraig have to travel sixty miles across Scotland to Dingwall on the east coast where they board for the week while attending school. At Little Gidding, itself a group dedicated to an ecologically acceptable way of life, questions were raised in the 1975 autumn newsletter about the appropriateness of the word 'self-sufficiency' and a suggestion was made that a better and less exclusive, indeed less possessive, phrase would be 'sufficiency through sharing'.

Where alternative ways of operating do emerge within the system, it is often in niches left by mass production which just cannot cater for certain more specialized services and commodities, often of a 'luxury' nature, such as candles, pottery, jewellery, and woodcarving. The Industrial Common Ownership Movement is in reality a drop in the ocean set against the massive national and even more massive multi-national companies at present using up the earth's resources on a vast scale.

The projects discussed, simply because they depend on specialized skills, whether in agriculture or in producing resins and plastics, attract workmen who are well trained or highly educated and therefore able to have a go at something new. There is thus an élitist feel to some projects where members, otherwise in a position to be fitted back into the mainstream, can for a while enjoy the privilege of doing their own thing. On the other hand it would be foolish to underestimate the personal and communal dedication, the readiness to endure considerable physical discomfort, and the sheer hard work required to set up these ventures.

Also problematical is the ability of these groups to survive very long on the basis of genuine all-round participation. There seems to be a slow but steady tendency for authoritarianism to set in, which can be fed either by intense identification with an ideal, sometimes of a religious nature, and a determination to see it survive at all costs (as with the Children of God), or for a *laissez-faire* situation to develop as some form of democratic control proves too demanding or too cumbersome (as with the Kingsway Community). The very *raison d'être* of moving apart from the system then disappears and the results may be technologically interesting – organic farming, constructing solar panels, and so on – but socially unremarkable.

These kinds of issue led Ralf Dahrendorf to criticize the 'misplaced romanticism which claims that "small" is not only "beautiful", but also feasible'. But there is another side to the coin: a view which, recognizing the fragile and sometimes exaggerated claims made for some of these experiments, still sees them as important models for what could be if only.... For where else can one look other than to delve deep into history or build castles in the air? At least something tangible is happening and is observable. People are now *seen* to exist in our time who do not go along with the norms of consumerism and affluence; there *are* those who challenge the ravaging of the land and seas; people *do* exist who refuse to take as inevitable the organization of work on authoritarian and socially divisive lines; and we *can* observe groups determined to throw off the weight of impersonal bureacratic structures. Seeds can grow, but no seeds means barren land.

Even where the small and the alternative are regarded as politically ineffective, the importance of these ventures in seeking to give a new dignity to man is recognized. Harry Newton, a founder member of the dominantly Marxist Institute of Workers' Control, writes: 'Socialism based on materialism appears to result in bureaucratic nightmare. Unless the economic and political structures of "Socialism" are imbued with the spirit of the Brotherhood of Man, they are barren and joyless.' He argues that such brotherhood should be very much the Christian's concern, not just to speak of but to live out. Alternative technology and alternative modes of organization in relation to work must in the end mean an alternative form of society. Many Christians, alongside others, in such enterprises as those I have described, have at least made a courageous and determined beginning, in practice not just in theory.

Robert L. Stivers · *The Sustainable Society*

Robert L. Stivers, *The Sustainable Society: Ethics and Economic Growth*, Westminster Press, Philadelphia 1976, pp.198–207, 222–24. Copyright © 1976 The Westminster Press. Used by permission

Neither technical nor political solutions *alone* will suffice. This is not to say technology and politics will play no role. They are key factors in any viable solution. Rather, it is to say that there must be a critical third component, a new world view involving a radical change of attitudes and values, before the sustainable society will become a reality.

This is a tall order. John Maynard Keynes, reflecting on his projection of future unlimited abundance leading to ever-increasing leisure, stated, 'I think with dread of the readjustment of habits and instincts of the ordinary man, bred into him for countless generations, which he may be asked to discard within a few decades.' Keynes's dread applies even more to the sustainable society. While critically important, the achievement of a new world view is the most difficult task of all.

The outlines and directions of a new world view or ethic are beginning to emerge. It is and must be a world view that reverses the present quasi-religious commitment to growth. It has two tasks: the criticism of the reigning ethic and the construction of an alternative. In these tasks Christians may find real opportunities to contribute.

1. One starting point is an appreciation of nature. Several recent philosophical and theological studies have started at precisely this point. Though they differ markedly in approach and content, they have in common both a deep appreciation of nature and a strong criticism of the now popular instrumental view of nature. Any theological or philosophical reconstruction must at least rectify the currently destructive imbalance that has resulted in Western culture from a too-narrow emphasis on man as the measure of all things.

Theologically, Christians have work to do if they are to play a significant role in this renewed appreciation of nature. Christians have neglected nature by a too-exclusive emphasis on God and man. Nature simply hasn't received equal time in the tradition; and even when it has, the attention received has mostly cast nature as an instrument of inferior status.

Not only has nature been neglected, but Christian views have played a significant, though ambiguous, part in the use and continuing importance of science, technology, and economic expansion. This is not so much a judgment on Christian thought as it is a frank awareness of its ideological role. Christians have given a boost to the material and ideological forces underlying economic growth through their general emphases, their themes of subduing and having dominion in Genesis, their desacralization of nature, and their natural theology. Moreover, this ideological role continues today, even though Christianity has only a marginal social influence and dominant attitudes toward nature have little explicit Christian content. If nothing else, Christians have in recent times acquiesced in the exploitation of nature.

One way for Christians to begin is by reassessing the dominion and stewardship themes in Genesis. To have dominion and subdue the earth meant one thing to the ancient Hebrews, who for all their faults could not be accused of endangering the global environment. In our time, when nature gods are no longer the threat they were to the Hebrews, the themes have become vehicles of pride and idolatry.

It is time to relax our subduing. 'Dominion' does not mean destruction. It implies loving stewardship, a meaning that a careful reading of the dominion texts in Genesis indicates was also intended by the Hebrews. 'Stewardship' is care for the earth and compassion for persons. And while the steward too easily becomes the slave overseer, this should not be an excuse for jettisoning this strong Biblical notion. Stewardship, for all its dangers, conveys man's actual relationship to nature. We are part of nature, yet stand outside of it, control it, and have the ability to interfere in it. Interfering in nature cannot be abolished. A return to nature in denial of transcendence will not solve our problems. The call of Genesis and the tradition is rather to care, to have compassion, and to exercise a just stewardship.

2. An implicit religion of growth with its accompanying exploitation of nature pervades our society. This fact should not be obscured by academic arguments, such as the question whether this religion of growth is a consequence or a betrayal of Christianity. The questioning of this implicit religion raises the specter of an ideological crisis. The way we have put our ideas together for several centuries is now cast into radical doubt. The crisis is profoundly religious, for there is an absence of religious sensitivity in our preoccupation with affluence. The perception of crisis reaches to our deepest self-identities.

This perception of crisis is heightened by the weakness in practice of alternative philosophies and religious understandings. Christians as well as humanists have bought into the religion of growth at a fearful cost – the loss of their own spiritual and prophetic traditions. Perhaps it is now time to view this implicit religion of growth as idolatrous, as another example in the long line of human pride. We have given free reign to avarice and exploitation and have divorced our deepest spiritual values from our activity in the world. Nor is it too much to view the environmental crisis and projections of future human suffering as warnings of God's impending judgment on our pride and idolatry.

Where do we turn? For Christians the answer is clear. The call of God is to repentance and reconciliation in Jesus Christ, a call which in the present circumstances is hard to hear and harder still to answer. Concretely it is a call to basics: to faith; to human appeals for food, clothing, shelter, and health; to liberating structures that provide opportunities for human cooperation and creativity; to the throwing off of enslaving forces of affluence. The cross of the present crisis is not the final word. Out of death comes new life. Jesus Christ has overthrown the enslaving powers. We are free to change our ways without fear of judgment, for God is with us.

3. Our view of nature and our religious understandings are only two of many subjects for reassessment. Attitudes toward work, consumption, and abundance must all be reconsidered. The myths surrounding science and technology must be punctured and new, more satisfying myths created. To counter the influence of the technostructure, nontechnical and noneconomic values must be raised up.

Here also we must reconsider mass production and the substitution of machine power for human labor. With E. F. Schumacher, perhaps we should have as one goal an 'intermediate technology,' which provides first-class tools to a system of production intensive in labor. Schumacher calls it 'technology with a human face.'

> The system of production by the masses mobilizes the priceless resources which are possessed by all human beings, their clever brains and skillful hands, and supports them with first-class tools. The technology of mass production is inherently violent, ecologically damaging, self-defeating in terms of non-renewable resources, and stultifying for the human person. The technology of production by the masses, making use of modern knowledge and experience, is conducive to decentralization, compatible with the laws of ecology, gentle in its use of scarce resources, and designed to serve the human person instead of making him the servant of machines (*Small is Beautiful*, ch.10).

That Schumacher's vision would be adaptable to all regions is not clear. Herman E. Daly thinks a serious problem in the industrialized nations will be how to share the work, or, on the other side of the coin, how to use the new leisure created by a slackening demand for labor. He assumes the continuation of advanced technology, although one scrubbed of its environmentally unsound elements. The difference between Schumacher and Daly confuses the picture. If human labor is emphasized, as in Schumacher, then many of the attitudes associated with the so-called Protestant work ethic will apply. Alternatively, if advanced technology dominates, then we will need to develop a leisure ethic and a work-sharing ethic. This picture is further confused by the obvious need for considerable labor to bring the sustainable society into being, Yet, while we retain many of our present hard-working attitudes, we will need to redirect them; to eliminate the obsessive aspects of some work habits, the felt need to work in order to consume, and the alienating character of much labor. To give order to this bewildering array of considerations is not possible at present. But the confusion does point to the concern of many that we will end up with a sense of meaninglessness where no one feels called to work for the common good. However unclear the work picture is, new consuming styles will be essential. The present waste of energy, food, and natural resources in the United States must end if there be any hope for the sustainable society. Schumacher says 'small is beautiful,' which points to the minimization policy we need. Not, 'How much can we get?' but, 'How little do we really need?' will be the consuming question. All of which implies a revolutionary new pattern of life with staggering implications in the United States.

4. Alternative solutions to the problems for which growth has historically provided the answers must be developed in this new world view. This means a face-to-face confrontation with the international and national realities of distribution, freedom and coercion, social strife, employment, and the potential consequences of a declining standard of living. This also means the development of an alternative world view to deal with these problems. Finally, this means a criticism of present cost accounting and changed perceptions of social costs.

But above all, ethical resources must be found for dealing with the increased domestic and international conflict which the equilibrium economy makes a very real possibility. Natural resource shortages and overcrowding alone will create numerous occasions for conflict. Equally significant, the continuation of present expenditures to support military establishments (over $200 billion annually throughout the world) and the continuation of present levels of international and domestic conflict would destroy the possibility of the sustainable society.

No more urgent task confronts us than that of shifting from conflict to cooperation. Human beings have always yearned for the day when swords would be beaten into plowshares, cheeks would instinctively be turned, and all persons would be good Samaritans. Today these images of perfect harmony need to be more than hopes. And while perfect peace is nowhere on the horizon, much ground can be covered before our ethical resources are exhausted.

Unfortunately, cooperation frequently means the sacrifice of immediate, personal gains for a hypothetically better future for all. Thus cooperation for Americans probably means reduced material consumption now so that poorer nations may grow, to the long-range betterment of all. This call to reduce consumption for the sake of cooperation is unprecedented. It taxes our ethical resources to the utmost.

In short, the sustainable society increases the likelihood of conflict at a time when present ethical and political resources are wrongly ordered to produce the peace which the society necessarily presupposes. Only a new world view involving both in thought and deed the widespread renunciation of force *and* injustice will be sufficient for this new situation.

5. Within the new world view there must occur a reversal of the current emphasis on quantity over quality, means over ends, structures over values, and the individual over the commons – all characteristic of the growth-advocacy position. Equally important, the new view will necessarily direct our attention to longer-range problems. What is needed is not a total shift from the present to the long-range, but a greater degree of balance. The new world view must consider the entire time span. We must, for example, weigh immediate benefits more carefully against long-range impacts and vice versa.

A concern for future generations is raised to much greater importance by the projections of the futurists. At present a vague and largely unarticulated concern exists. The new world view must go far beyond just a vague concern. It must point to the personhood of our grandchildren, to the need for a heightened stewardship in an enlarged definition of the situation, and to the insensitivity produced now by the neglect of the future.

Here the proponents of the new may find help in the current trend toward theologies of the future. We do not mean those theologies which seek a simple solution to the world's problems, undercutting ·the will to create more just institutions. Rather, we are referring to those which face the full range of possible responses to God's love and attempt to point concretely to where God may be at work. Too often much of God's work is overlooked because we fail to flesh out our theologies with real possibilities.

From a theological standpoint we affirm that God will be at work in the future through love to bring into being more just social institutions and new relationships of persons to nature. But God's work of justice and love is always concretely embodied – as, for example, in the incarnation. Indeed, we are called to respond in acts of love, not in abstract affirmations.

Thus it is not sufficient merely to affirm that God will be at work in the future. It is also necessary to make concrete, though *tentative*, judgments about his presence. It is necessary to outline tentative utopias that envision new societies and new relationships to nature as the material embodiments of abstract eschatology. For the new world view this means serious consideration of the sustainable society as one possible embodiment of God's love.

Equally important is the development and communication of a persuasive basis for hope. The past two centuries have seen a close link between hope, optimism, and a sense of vitality on the one hand, and material increase on the other. Because of this link, the specter of the end of the lode may easily lead to pessimism, nihilism, and 'loss of nerve.' It is of little use to say that material increase has been a false, even idolatrous, goal. The fact is, this link has been strong, and the breaking of it is fraught with complications.

The new world view will therefore have to develop a new basis for hope, optimism, and vitality. And to use the word 'new' is not to suggest that an entirely original ethic must be carved out of virgin timber. Ample resources are available within the Christian tradition to provide a sound basis. The word 'new' would indicate the shifting away from the present world view, which is dominated by economic and technical considerations.

6. Finally, even if the futurists are wrong, there are compelling reasons to shift from a 'growth' to a 'sustainable' world view. Many elements of the sustainable society are desirable in their own right. They are needed correctives for present social injustice and callousness, and for the tendency to give primary attention to economic and technologically based values. The world view outlined here is therefore not merely an antidote for the problems of limits; just as important, it is a suggestive new ethical direction. The proponents of the sustainable society would do well to insist, as their first priority, that the new society offer at least as many possibilities as problems.

We believe that God's love and our response will provide the resources to overcome the forces of destruction even in the most threatening situations. This does not mean a future of cornucopian abundance. Nor does it mean that we can sit back and let God do it. God simply doesn't work that way. We are free, free to affirm or deny Christ's lordship. God does not intervene like the Lone Ranger or Superman to reconcile what our denial of him has alienated. God's mercy and love are effective in persons and communities only with confession, repentance, and acceptance of new life. God now calls us to repentance and new direction. His call is to throw off the determinism of the past and the rigid, encrusted structures of the present. His call is to an open future where we can be assured he will be present.

In the context of our present discussion, this call is to three tasks: (1) to slow down and redirect the present narrow thrust for growth; (2) to determine our economic goals in terms of environmental soundness and human welfare and to act responsibly on this decision; (3) to make the possibilities of the future imaginatively concrete. We should have no illusions about bringing in the perfect society. Alienation will continue. Freedom and creativity will be tested to their limits. Problems will abound. Nonetheless, the call is clear. We are called to use our limited freedom and imagination in loving response to the love of God, not to become mired in the problems and to lose sight of the possibilities.

We affirm that the future is full of possibilities and hope. Some may despair at the prospects. Others may choose to escape into easy answers, strange cults, or simply into sloth. In contrast to despair and escape, the faithful response is a new spurt of creative imagination, a new effort to pull concrete possibilities out of an open future. Without vision there is little hope for higher levels of love, justice, and fulfillment.

The sustainable society is much more than a proposal to avoid catastrophe. Given certain qualifications, it is the vision we need to overcome injustice to persons and insensitivity to nature. For the church it may even be the opportunity to break its present affair with mammon and to review its commitment to persons, nature, and God. For humanists and Christians alike the new society could provide the occasion for dealing with a number of ethical problems now ignored in our single-minded pursuit of growth.

The sustainable society is not a bleak last resort or a bad vision challenging our hard-won material security. Our forefathers managed to survive without great abundance, and we have the enviable advantage of several centuries of discovery and invention. We are not headed back into the Dark Ages. Invention and discovery will not end with the thrust for growth. The sustainable society is a viable and even desirable alternative to the present growth economy and ethic.

Seeing the sustainable society as a positive possibility significantly enlarges the question, Is growth desirable? The sustainable society offers a new alternative, given three critical provisions: (1) the availability of basic material necessities to all; (2) a far more equitable distribution both internationally and domestically; and (3) a political process characterized by openness and not by repression. Now the question of desirability can be stated as a choice between growth and equilibrium. No longer need we ask whether growth is desirable or undesirable, but which is more desirable, a growth economy and ethic such as we have now with first-aid modifications, or the sustainable society?

E. F. Schumacher · *The Home-Comers*

E. F. Schumacher, *Small is Beautiful*, Harper & Row, NY, and Blond & Briggs 1973; Abacus 1975, pp.128, 129–30, 246–48

As Gandhi said, the poor of the world cannot be helped by mass production, only by production by the masses. The system of *mass production*, based on sophisticated, highly capital-intensive, high energy-input dependent, and human labour-saving technology, pre-supposes that you are already rich, for a great deal of capital investment is needed to establish one single workplace. The system of *production by the masses* mobilises the priceless resources which are possessed by all human beings, their clever brains and skilful hands, *and supports them with first-class tools.* The technology of *mass production* is inherently violent, ecologically damaging, self-defeating in terms of non-renewable resources, and stultifying for the human person. The technology of *production by the masses*, making use of the best of modern knowledge and experience, is conducive to decentralisation, compatible with the laws of ecology, gentle in its use of scarce resources, and designed to serve the human person instead of making him the servant of machines. I have named it *intermediate technology* to signify that it is vastly superior to the primitive technology of bygone ages but at the same time much simpler, cheaper, and freer than the super-technology of the rich. One can also call it self-help technology, or democratic or people's technology – a technology to which everybody can gain admittance and which is not reserved to those already rich and powerful. It will be more fully discussed in later chapters.

I think we can already see the conflict of attitudes which will decide our future. On the one side, I see the people who think they can cope with our threefold crisis by the methods current, only more so; I call them the people of the forward stampede. On the other side, there are people in search of a new life-style, who seek to return to certain basic truths about man and his world; I call them home-comers. Let us admit that the people of the forward stampede, like the devil, have all the best tunes or at least the most popular and familiar tunes. You cannot stand still, they say; standing still means going down; you must go forward; there is nothing wrong with modern technology except that it is as yet incomplete; let us complete it. Dr Sicco Mansholt, one of the most prominent chiefs of the European Economic Community, may be quoted as a typical representative of this group. 'More, further, quicker, richer,' he says, 'are the watchwords of present-day society.' And he thinks we must help people to adapt 'for there is no alternative'. This is the authentic voice of the forward stampede, which talks in much the same tone as Dostoyevsky's Grand Inquisitor: 'Why have you come to hinder us?' They point to the population explosion and to the possibilities of world hunger. Surely, we must take our flight forward and not be fainthearted. If people start protesting and revolting, we shall have to have more police and have them better equipped. If there is trouble with the environment, we shall need more stringent laws against pollution, and faster economic growth to pay for anti-pollution measures. If there are problems about natural resources, we shall turn to synthetics; if there are problems about fossil fuels, we shall move from slow reactors to fast breeders and from fission to fusion. There *are* no insoluble problems. The slogans of the people of the forward stampede burst into the newspaper headlines every day with the message, 'a breakthrough a day keeps the crisis at bay'.

And what about the other side? This is made up of people who are deeply convinced that technological development has taken a wrong turn and needs to be redirected. The term 'home-comer' has, of course, a religious connotation. For it takes a good deal of courage to say 'no' to the fashions and fascinations of the age and to question the presuppositions of a civilisation which appears destined to conquer the whole world; the requisite strength can be derived only from deep convictions. If it were derived from nothing more than fear of the future, it would be likely to disappear at the decisive moment. The genuine 'home-comer' does not have the best tunes, but he has the most exalted text, nothing less than the Gospels. For him, there could not be a more concise statement of his situation, of *our* situation, than the parable of the prodigal son. Strange to say, the Sermon on the Mount gives pretty precise instructions on how to construct an outlook that could lead to an Economics of Survival.

How blessed are those who know that they are poor:
the Kingdom of Heaven is theirs.
How blessed are the sorrowful;
they shall find consolation.
How blessed are those of a gentle spirit;
they shall have the earth for their possession.
How blessed are those who hunger and thirst to see right prevail;
they shall be satisfied;
How blessed are the peacemakers;
God shall call them his sons.

It may seem daring to connect these beatitudes with matters of technology and economics. But may it not be that we are in trouble precisely because we have failed for so long to make this connection? It is not difficult to discern what these beatitudes may mean for us today:

We are poor, not demigods.
We have plenty to be sorrowful about, and are not emerging into a golden age.
We need a gentle approach, a non-violent spirit, and small is beautiful.
We must concern ourselves with justice and see right prevail.
And all this, only this, can enable us to become peacemakers.

The home-comers base themselves upon a different picture of man from that which motivates the people of the forward stampede. It would be very superficial to say that the the latter believe in 'growth' while the former do not. In a sense, everybody believes in growth, and rightly so, because growth is an essential feature of life. The whole point, however, is to give to the idea of growth a qualitative determination; for there are always many things that ought to be growing and many things that ought to be diminishing.

Equally, it would be very superficial to say that the home-comers do not believe in progress, which also can be said to be an essential feature of all life. The whole point is to determine what constitutes progress. And the home-comers believe that the direction which modern technology has taken and is continuing to pursue – towards ever-greater size, every-higher speeds, and ever-increased violence, in defiance of all laws of natural harmony – is the opposite of progress. Hence the call for taking stock and finding a new orientation. The stocktaking indicates that we are destroying our very basis of existence, and the reorientation is based on remembering what human life is really about.

In the excitement over the unfolding of his scientific and technical powers, modern man has built a system of production that ravishes nature and a type of society that mutilates man. If only there were more and more wealth, everything else, it is thought, would fall into place. Money is considered to be all-powerful; if it could not actually buy non-material values, such as justice, harmony, beauty or even health, it could circumvent the need for them or compensate for their loss. The development of production and the acquisition of wealth have thus become the highest goals of the modern world in relation to which all other goals, no matter how much lip-service may still be paid to them, have come to take second place. The highest goals require no justification; all secondary goals have finally to justify themselves in terms of the service their attainment renders to the attainment of the highest.

This is the philosophy of materialism, and it is this philosophy – or metaphysic – which is now being challenged by events. There has never been a time, in any society in any part of the world, without its sages and teachers to challenge materialism and plead for a different order of priorities. The languages have differed, the symbols have varied, yet the message has always been the same: 'seek ye *first* the kingdom of God, and these things (the material things which you also need) shall be *added* unto you.' They shall be added, we are told, here on earth where we need them, not simply in an after-life beyond our imagination. Today, however, this message reaches us not solely from the sages and saints but from the actual course of physical events. It speaks to us in the language of terrorism, genocide, breakdown, pollution, exhaustion. We live, it seems in a unique period of convergence. It is becoming apparent that there is not only a promise but also a threat in those astonishing words about the kingdom of God – the threat that 'unless you seek first the kingdom, these other things, which you also need, will cease to be available to you' . . .

We shrink back from the truth if we believe that the destructive forces of the modern world can be 'brought under control' simply by mobilising more resources – of wealth, education, and research – to fight pollution, to preserve wildlife, to discover new sources of energy, and to arrive at more effective agreements on peaceful coexistence. Needless to say, wealth, education, research, and many other things are needed for any civilisation, but what is most needed today is a revision of the ends which these means are meant to serve. And this implies, above all else, the development of a life-style which accords to material things their proper, legitimate place, which is secondary and not primary.

The 'logic of production' is neither the logic of life nor that of society. It is a small and subservient part of both. The destructive forces unleashed by it cannot be brought under control, unless the 'logic of production' itself is brought under control – so that destructive forces cease to be unleashed. It is of little use trying to suppress terrorism if the production of deadly devices continues to be deemed a legitimate employment of man's creative powers. Nor can the fight against pollution be successful if the patterns of production and consumption continue to be of a scale, a complexity, and a degree of violence which, as is becoming more and more apparent, do not fit into the laws of the universe, to which man is just as much subject as the rest of creation. Equally, the chance of mitigating the rate of resource depletion or of bringing harmony into the relationships between those in possession of wealth and power and those without is non-existent as long as there is no idea anywhere of enough being good and more than enough being of evil.

It is a hopeful sign that some awareness of these deeper issues is gradually – if exceedingly cautiously – finding expression even in some official and semi-official utterances. A report, written by a committee at the request of the Secretary of State for the Environment, talks about buying time during which technologically developed societies have an opportunity 'to revise their values and to change their political objectives'. It is a matter of 'moral choices', says the report, 'no amount of calculation can alone provide the answers.... The fundamental questioning of conventional values by young people all over the world is a symptom of the widespread unease with which our industrial civilisation is increasingly regarded.' Pollution must be brought under control and mankind's population and consumption of resources must be steered towards a permanent and sustainable equilibrium. 'Unless this is done, sooner or later – and some believe that there is little time left – the downfall of civilisation will not be a matter of science fiction. It will be the experience of our children and grandchildren.'

But how is it to be done? What are the 'moral choices'? Is it just a matter, as the report also suggests, of deciding 'how much we are willing to pay for clean surroundings'? Mankind has indeed a certain freedom of choice: it is not bound by trends, by the 'logic of production', or by any other fragmentary logic. But it is bound by truth. Only in the service of truth is perfect freedom, and even those who today ask us 'to free our imagination from bondage to the existing system' fail to point the way to the recognition of truth.

Biographical Notes

Tissa Balasuriya, o.m.i., read theology in Colombo, Sri Lanka and later in Rome. He has been visiting lecturer in many countries in Asia, Europe and also in the United States. He was formerly Rector of Aquinas University College, Colombo, and since 1969 has been chaplain to the Asian Catholic Student Federation and Director of the Centre for Society and Religion, Colombo. He has written extensively on ecumenism, mission, human development, spirituality and poverty and social justice.

José Míguez Bonino was born in Santa Fé, Argentina in 1924. He read theology at the Faculty of Protestant Theology, University of Buenos Aires, before taking a master's degree in teaching at Emery University. He was awarded the degree of ThD from Union Theological Seminary, New York in 1960. He has served in many parts of Argentina as a pastor of the Evangelical Methodist Church. From 1954–70 he taught in the Faculty of Protestant Theology at Buenos Aires and is now Dean of Post-Graduate Studies at the Institute of Higher Theological Studies.

Arthur M. Brazier is pastor of the Apostolic Church of God in Woodlawn, one of the most densely populated areas of Chicago. He is an officer in The Woodlawn Organization, a community organization set up in 1959 through the initiative of the clergy of four different denominations in the area.

David Clark was born in Nottingham in 1934 and read history at the University of Oxford before going on to study theology in Birmingham. He worked as a Methodist minister in Sheffield and Greenwich. He holds a PhD in sociology from the University of Sheffield and lectures in community and youth work at Westhill College, Birmingham.

Sheila Collins is a social activist and writer on feminism, socialism, theology and the liberation movements of the Third World. She was born in Toronto, Canada, in 1940 and read English literature at Carleton College before taking her master's degree at Columbia University. She has also studied Christian education at Union Theological Seminary, New York. Ms Collins has taught courses on women and religion and on capitalism and Christianity at Union and other centres, including the Pacific School of Religion. In addition to her prolific writings in these areas, she has written poems which have recently been collected and published. At present she is working for the ecumenical Joint Strategy and Action Committee, based in New York.

Mary Daly was born in Schenectady, NY, in 1928 and studied at the College of St Rose, Albany and the Catholic University of America before taking her PhD at Notre Dame. She taught theology and philosophy at Cardinal Cushing College, Brookline, Mass. before spending seven years in Switzerland doing post-graduate study and teaching. She was awarded the degrees of STL, DrTheol and PhD from the University of Fribourg. Since 1966 Professor Daly has taught at Boston College and in 1973 was Harry Emerson Fosdick Visiting Professor at Union Theological Seminary, New York. At present she has a Rockefeller Foundation Humanities grant to enable her to research her next major work, to be entitled, *Gyn/Ecology: The Metaethics of Radical Feminism*. Professor Daly is on the advisory board of *Women's Studies International Quarterly*.

Enrique Dussell was born in La Paz in 1934. He is a Professor of History and Philosophy at the Latin American Pastoral Institute (IPLA) which is a branch of CELAM at Quito, Ecuador. He is also Professor of Ethics at the University of Cuyo.

Alfredo Fierro is Director of the University Institute of Theology, Madrid.

Ian M. Fraser was born in Forres, Morayshire in 1917 and read arts and theology at the University of Edinburgh. He became a member of the Iona Community and was one of the pioneers of the worker-priest movement in industry before going to the dockyard town of Rosyth in 1948 as a parish minister. At this time he took his PhD from Edinburgh. Dr Fraser was invited to set up and organize the Scottish Churches House in Dunblane. In 1969 he went to Geneva to work for the World Council of Churches, first with responsibility for 'Laity Studies' and then as director for the programme on 'Participation and Change'. In 1973 he was appointed Dean and Head of the Department of Mission at the Selly Oak Colleges, Birmingham.

Walter J. Hollenweger was born in Antwerp in 1927 and studied at the universities of Zurich and Basel before graduating with a DrTheol from Zurich in 1966. From 1965–71 he was Executive Secretary of the World Council of Churches. Since 1971 he has been Professor of Mission, University of Birmingham. He is probably the world authority on pentecostalism.

Ivan Illich was born in Vienna in 1926. He read theology and philosophy at the Gregorian University in Rome and took his PhD in history at the University of Salzburg. He worked for a time in an Irish-Puerto Rican church in New York before serving from 1956–60 as Vice-Rector of the Catholic University of Puerto Rico. He was co-founder of the Center for Intercultural Documentation in Cuernavaca. He is widely known for his criticism of Western attitudes to schooling and medicine.

Alistair Kee was born in 1937 in Alexandria, Dunbartonshire and read arts and theology at the University of Glasgow. After joining the Iona Community he went to New York and took his master's and doctor's degrees at Union Theological Seminary. In 1965 he began teaching at the University College of Rhodesia, a few months before the white rebellion against Britain (UDI). From 1967–76 he taught at the University of Hull and is now Head of the Department of Religious Studies, University of Glasgow.

Yong-Bock Kim read theology in Japan before going on to work under Richard Shaull at Princeton, where he graduated with a PhD in 1970, his dissertation being on 'Peoples' Revolution in Korean History'. He is co-editor of *Documents on the Struggle for Democracy in Korea* and is at present on the staff of the National Christian Council, Seoul, Korea, with responsibility for Documentation. He was previously on the staff of Sophia University, Tokyo, in International Studies.

Kosuke Koyama is senior lecturer in Religious Studies, University of Otago, Dunedin, New Zealand. He was a Japanese Kyodan missionary to the Church of Christ in Thailand, 1960–68, teaching at Thailand Theological Seminary in Chiengmai. From 1968–74 he was executive director of the Association of Theological Schools in South East Asia, Dean of the South East Asia Graduate School of Theology, and editor of the *South East Asia Journal of Theology*, with headquarters in Singapore.

Johannes B. Metz was born in Welluck, Germany in 1928 and was ordained as a Catholic priest in 1954. He studied at the Universities of Innsbruck and Munich and is a doctor of philosophy and theology. He is now Professor of Fundamental Theology at the University of Munster.

José Porfirio Miranda was born in Mexico and studied economics at the universities of Munich and Munster before gaining his Licentiate in Biblical Studies from the Biblical Institute in Rome in 1967. He has been a Professor of Mathematics at the Institute de Ciencias and Professor of Economic Theory at the Institutio Tecnologico in Guadalajara, Professor of Philosophy at the Institutio Regionale (Chihuahua), Professor of the Philosophy of Law at the National University and Professor of Exegesis at the Institutio Libre de Filosofia in Mexico City. He has been closely involved with workers' and students' groups and lives in the working class area of Ciudad Netzahualcoyotl.

Jürgen Moltmann is Professor of Systematic Theology at the University of Tübingen. He studied at the University of Göttingen and has been visiting professor at Duke University. He was born in 1926 and his theological thinking has been bound up with his experience of war, the reconstruction of Germany and the radical protest movement of the late 1960s. He has been active in projects associated with the World Council of Churches.

Rosemary R. Ruether was born in Minneapolis in 1936 and graduated with an MA and PhD in classics and patristics from Clarement Graduate School. She taught at both Harvard and Yale Divinity Schools and for ten years has been teaching at Howard University School of Religion, Washington, DC.

At present she is Georgia Harkness Professor of Applied Theology, Garrett-Evangelical Theological Seminary, Evanston. Professor Ruether is an editor of *Christianity and Crisis* and the *Ecumenist*.

E. F. Schumacher was born in Germany and studied economics at Oxford as a Rhodes Scholar. At the age of 22 he taught at Columbia University. He gained practical experience as a businessman, farmer and journalist, but returned to Oxford during the Second World War and later served as economic adviser with the British Control Commission in Germany until 1950. For the next twenty years he was economic adviser to the National Coal Board. He was the originator of the concept of 'intermediate technology' and has often been consulted by governments of the developing countries. He was founder-chairman of the Intermediate Technology Development Group in London and Director of the Scott-Bader Institute.

Juan Luis Segundo was born in 1925 in Uruguay. He is a Jesuit and has been awarded doctorates in theology and sociology from Louvain and Paris. He is Director of the Pedro Fabbro Institute of Socio-religious Research in Montevideo.

Robert L. Stivers was born in Cincinnati in 1940, and studied at Yale University before becoming an Officer in the US Navy. In 1969 he was awarded a Travelling Fellowship from Union Theological Seminary, and afterwards studied at Columbia University, where he gained his PhD in 1973. Since 1974 he has been Assistant Professor of Religion at Pacific Lutheran University.

Carlos Talavera is Director of the Social Secretariat of the Catholic archdiocese of Mexico City.

The Theological Writing Collective of the Christians for National Liberation. For security reasons it is not possible to disclose the identity of the members of the group. If this underlines the risks taken by the members in formulating their views it also emphasizes the fact that this theology is not a personal or eccentric matter but reflects the faith and experience of many Christians in the Philippines today.

Josef Widyatmadja studied at Duta Wacana Seminary in Jogjakarta, Indonesia, graduating with a BD in 1971 and STh in 1975. In 1972 he trained at the Urban Industrial Mission, Jakarta and in the following year at the Institute of Social Order, Manila in the Philippines. From 1973–75 he was pastor to an urban congregation in Solo, Java, where he still works, and established the Social Welfare Guidance Foundation, assisting poor communities towards their self-organization. Since 1975 he has worked in a training capacity for Community Organization for Indonesia, sponsored by the Asian Committee for Peoples' Organization, a joint Catholic–Protestant organization active throughout Asia.

Bibliography

The following works in English are grouped for convenience under five headings. While this arrangement is useful for reference it is quite artificial, since all works included contribute to the central concerns of political theology.

Political Theology

Assman, H., *Practical Theology of Liberation*, Search Press 1975
  Theology for a Nomad Church, Orbis Books, Maryknoll 1976
Coles, R., *A Spectacle unto the World: The Catholic Worker Movement*, Viking Press, NY 1973
Dewart, L., *Christianity and Revolution: The Lesson of Cuba*, Herder & Herder, NY 1963
Dussel, E., 'Domination-Liberation: A New Approach', *Concilium*, vol. 6, no. 10, 1974, pp.34–56
  History and the Theology of Liberation, Orbis Books, Maryknoll 1976
Eagleson, J. (ed.), *Christians and Socialism*, Orbis Books, Maryknoll 1975
Galilea, S., 'Liberation as an Encounter with Politics and Contemplation', *Concilium*, vol. 6, no. 10, 1974, pp.19–33
Gremillion, J., *The Gospel of Peace and Justice*, Orbis Books, Maryknoll 1975
Herzog, F., 'Political Theology', *Christian Century*, 22 July 1969, pp.975–78
Kee, A. (ed.), *A Reader in Political Theology*, SCM Press 1974
  Seeds of Liberation, SCM Press 1973
Klaiber, J. L., *Religion and Revolution in Peru, 1824–1976*, Univ. of Notre Dame Press, Indiana 1977
Lane, D. (ed.), *Liberation Theology*, Gill and Macmillan, Dublin 1977
Metz, J. B., *Theology of the World*, Herder & Herder, NY, and Search Press 1969

Miller, W. D., *A Harsh and Dreadful Love: Dorothy Day and the Catholic Worker Movement*, Darton, Longman & Todd 1973

Moltmann, J., *The Church in the Power of the Spirit*, SCM Press 1977
The Crucified God, SCM Press 1975
'An Open Letter to José Miguez-Bonino', *Christianity and Crisis*, March 1976, p.60
'Political Theology', *Theology Today*, vol. 28, 1971, pp.6–23

Oelmüller, W., 'Ethics and Politics Today: Philosophical Foundations', *Concilium*, vol. 4, 1968, pp.22–28

Petulla, J., *Christian Political Theology*, Orbis Books, Maryknoll 1972

Prien, H. J., 'Liberation and Development in Latin America', *Lutheran World*, vol. 20, 1973, pp.114–32

Rostagno, S., *Essays in the New Testament: A 'materialist' approach*, WSCF, Geneva 1976

Ruis, J. G., *The New Creation: Marxist and Christian?*, Orbis Books, Maryknoll 1976

Rutgers, J., 'Church-State Confrontation in Brazil' in *Repression in Latin America*, ed. Jerman, W., Spokesman Books 1975

Schmidt, H., 'Lines of Political Action in Contemporary Liturgy', *Concilium*, vol. 2, no. 10, 1974, pp.13–33

Schutz, R., *Struggle and Contemplation*, SPCK 1974

Segundo, J. L., *The Liberation of Theology*, Orbis Books, Maryknoll, and Gill & Macmillan, Dublin 1977
A Theology for Artisans of a New Humanity (5 vols), Orbis Books, Maryknoll 1972–74

Soelle, D., *Political Theology*, Fortress Press, Philadelphia 1974

Stringfellow, W., *An Ethic for Christians and Other Aliens in a Strange Land*, World Books, Waco, Texas 1973

Winter, D., *Hope and Captivity: The Prophetic Church in Latin America*, Epworth Press 1977

Pentecostal Conscience

Brazier, A., *Black Self-Determination: The Story of the Woodlawn Organization*, Eerdmans Pub. Co., Grand Rapids 1969

Clark, S. B., *Building Christian Communities: A Strategy for Pastoral Renewal*, Ave Maria Press, Notre Dame, Indiana 1972

d'Opinay, C. L., *Haven of the Masses: A Study of the Pentecostal Movement in Chile*, Lutterworth Press 1969

Fahey, S. M., *Charismatic Social Action: Reflection/Resource Manual*, Paulist Press, NJ 1977

Haufe, C. M., 'Young Charismatics in Eastern Germany', *Lutheran World*, vol. 22, 1975, pp.340–43

Harper, M., *A New Way of Living*, Hodder & Stoughton 1973

Hollenweger, W. J., 'African Charisma', *International Review of Mission*, vol. 61, 1972, pp.196–201

'Pentecostalism and Black Power', *Theology Today*, vol. 30, no. 3, 1973, pp. 228–38

Pentecost Between Black and White, Christian Journals, Belfast 1974

'The Social and Ecumenical Significance of Pentecostal Liturgy', *Studia Liturgia*, vol. 8, no. 1971–72, pp.207–15

Kami, Peter et al (eds), *Pentecost and Politics*, Movement Pamphlet No. 21, SCM Publications, Dublin 1975

Martin, R., *Sent by the Spirit*, Paulist Press, NJ 1976

MacNutt, F., 'Pentecostals and Social Justice', *New Covenant*, vol. 2, no. 5, 1972

O'Mara, P., 'Social Action', *New Covenant*, vol. 2, nos 4–5, 1972

Pulkingham, B., & Harper, J., *Sound of Living Waters*, Hodder & Stoughton 1975

Pulkingham, G., *Gathered for Power*, Hodder & Stoughton 1973

Randall, J., *In God's Providence*, Living Flame Press, Locust Valley, NY 1972

Sullivan, E., 'Can the Pentecostal Movement Renew the Churches?', *Study Encounter*, vol. 8, 1972

Schonfield, H., *The Pentecostal Revolution*, Macdonald & James 1974

Feminist Perspective

Buren van, N., *The Subversion of Women as Practiced by Churches: Witch Hunters and Other Sexists*, Westminster Press, Philadelphia 1973

Burns, J. E. *God as Woman, Woman as God*, Paulist Press, NJ 1973

Daly, M., *Beyond God the Father*, Beacon Press, Boston 1973

The Church and the Second Sex, Harper & Row, NY 1968

Fiorenza, E. S., 'Feminist Theology as a Critical Theology of Liberation', *Theological Studies*, vol. 36, no. 4, 1975, pp.605–26

Ermath, M. S., *Adam's Fractured Rib*, Fortress Press, Philadelphia 1970

Hageman, A. L. (ed.), *Sexist Religion and Women in the Church*, Association Press, NY 1974

Hogan, D. C., *Woman and the Christian Experience: Feminist Ideology, Christian Theology and Spirituality*, Boston Univ. Graduate School Ph.D thesis 1975

Moore, Basil et al, *Theology and Sexual Politics*, Movement Pamphlet No. 8, SCM Publications, Dublin 1973

Richardson, H., *Nun, Witch, Playmate*, Harper & Row, NY 1971

Ruether, R. R., & Bianchi, E., *From Machismo to Mutuality: Man-Woman Liberation in America*, Paulist Press, NJ 1975

Ruether, R. R. (ed.), *Images of Women in the Jewish and Christian Traditions*, Simon & Schuster, NY 1973
(ed.), *Religion and Sexism*, Simon & Schuster, NY 1973
Liberation Theology, Paulist Press, NJ 1972
New Woman/New Earth, Seabury Press, NY 1975

Russell, L. M., *Human Liberation in a Feminist Perspective – A Theology*, Westminster Press, Philadelphia 1974

Trible, P., 'Depatriarchalizing in Biblical Interpretation', *Journal of the American Academy of Religion*, XLI, 1973, pp.31–34

Voices from Asia

Anderson, G. H. (ed.), *Asian Voices in Christian Theology*, Orbis Books, Maryknoll 1976
Christ and Crisis in South-East Asia, Friendship Press, NY 1967

Arevalo, C. G., 'On the Theology of the Signs of the Times' in *Filipino in the Seventies*, R. Deats and V. Gorospe (eds), New Day, Manila 1973

Avila, C. (ed.), *Peasant Theology*, WSCF 1975

Balasuriya, T., *The Church and the Asian Revolution*, Centre for Society and Religion, Colombo 1972
Development of its Poor through the Civilizing of the Rich, National Council of Churches, Christchurch, NZ 1972

Bulatao, J. (ed.), *Split Level Christianity*, Ateneo, Manila 1966

Briedenstein, G., *Christians and Social Justice: Modern Theology, Socio-Political Problems and Community Organization in Korea*, Korean Student Christian Federation 1974

Ellwood, D. J. (ed.), *What Asian Christians are Thinking*, New Day, Manila 1976

IDOC, *An Asian Theology of Liberation in the Philippines*, IDOC, Rome 1973

Kim Chi Ha, *The Cry of the People*, Autumn Press 1975

Koyama, K., *No Handle on the Cross*, SCM Press 1976
Waterbuffalo Theology, SCM Press 1974

Simatupang, T. B., 'The Confessing Church in Contemporary Asia', *South-east Asia Journal of Theology*, vol. 8, no. 3, 1967

Torre, E. de la, 'The Passion, Death and Resurrection of the Petty-Bourgeois Christian', *The Future of the Missionary Enterprise*, IDOC 1973

Widjaja, A., 'Beggarly Theology', *South-east Asia Journal of Theology*, vol. 14, no. 2, 1973–74

Ecology and Community

Alpers, K. P., 'Starting Point for an Ecological Theology: a bibliographical survey', *New Theology*, no. 8, 1971

Barbour, I. G. (ed.), *Earth Might Be Fair*, Prentice-Hall, NJ 1972

Bonifazi, C., *A Theology of Things: a study of man in his physical environment*, Lippincott, Philadelphia 1967

Clark, D., *Basic Communities*, SPCK 1977

Cobb, J. B., *Is It Too Late? A Theology of Ecology*, Bruce Books, CA 1972

Derr, T. S., *Ecology and Human Liberation*, WSCF 1976

Derrick, C., *The Delicate Creation*, Tom Stacey 1972

Ecologist, 'A Blueprint for Survival', *The Ecologist*, vol. 2, no. 1, 1972

Elder, F., *Crisis in Eden*, Abingdon Press, Nashville 1970

Fraser, I. M., *The Fire Runs*, SCM Press 1974

Grail, The, *A Society of Lay People*, The Grail Community 1974

Hayward, A., *Planet Earth's Last Hope*, Marshall, Morgan & Scott 1973

Haughton, R., *On Trying to be Human*, Geoffrey Chapman 1966

Heiss, R. L., & McInnis, N. F. (eds), *Can Man Care for the Earth?*, Abingdon Press, Nashville 1971

Ineson, G., *Community Journey*, Sheed & Ward 1956

Kayson, C., 'The Computer that Printed out Wolf', *Foreign Affairs*, vol. 50, no. 4, 1972

Lockley, A., *Christian Communes*, SCM Press 1976

Meadows, D. H. et al, *The Limits to Growth*, Universe Books, NY, and Earth Island Ltd 1972

Montefiore, H., *Can Man Survive?*, Fontana Books 1970

Neuhaus, R., *In Defense of People: Ecology and the Seduction of Radicalism*, Macmillan, NY 1971

Plant, R., *Community and Ideology*, Routledge & Kegan Paul 1974

Rigby, A., *Alternative Realities*, Routledge & Kegan Paul 1974

Communes in Britain, Routledge & Kegan Paul 1974

Santmire, H. P., *Brother Earth: Nature, God and Ecology in Time of Crisis*, Thomas Nelson, Camden, NJ 1970

Schumacher, E. F., *Small is Beautiful*, Blond & Briggs 1973; Abacus 1974

Shinn, R. L., 'Ethics and the Family of Man' in *This Little Planet*, ed. M. Hamilton, Scribners' Sons, NY 1970

Stivers, R. L., *The Sustainable Society*, Westminster Press, Philadelphia 1976

Taylor, J. V., *Enough is Enough*, SCM Press 1975

Ward, B., & Dubos, R., *Only One Earth*, Penguin Books, 1972

White, L., 'The Historical Roots of our Ecological Crisis', *Science*, 155, 1967, pp.1203–7